TATTOO ART

A PHOTOGRAPHIC SOURCEBOOK

Doralba Picerno

Capella

This edition published in 2012 by Arcturus Publishing Limited
26/27 Bickels Yard, 151–153 Bermondsey Street,
London SE1 3HA

ISBN: 978-1-84858-919-3
AD002316N

Printed in Singapore

TATTOO ART

CONTENTS

6
INTRODUCTION

10
PURE DESIGN

20
FAMOUS FACES

30
FANTASY WORLD

42
NATURAL WORLD

58
GETTING AWAY

66
LOVE OBJECTS

80
THE LIGHTER SIDE

92
SYMBOLISM

112
FUSION

TOP LEFT
A photographic portrait of a much loved rock icon: Kurt Cobain by Andy Engel, Andy's Tattoo, Kitzingen, Germany.

TOP RIGHT
A colourful and detailed animal portrait by Jo Harrison, Modern Body Art, Birmingham, UK.

BOTTOM LEFT
A sugar skull girl holding a sugar skull: a homage to folk Mexican imagery by Tony B, UK.

BOTTOM RIGHT
Hand-poked tattoo by Sakura Avalon, UK.

INTRODUCTION

I remember a time, not so long ago, when tattoos were regarded with suspicion and the people sporting them were invariably assumed to lead 'colourful' lives. How things change! Today tattoos have lost their stigma and are essential accessories for many followers of street fashion. While a visible tattoo might hamper your chance of working in a bank, it will not necessarily affect your employment prospects elsewhere. When Lady Gaga feels compelled to mimic Zombie Boy's well-known facial tattoo in one of her videos, it is clear that permanent skin designs have seeped undeniably into the mainstream.

One of the most interesting aspects of modern tattooing is the way in which its designs have evolved to reflect the zeitgeist. As tattoo practice has become more widespread, techniques have become more refined, allowing artists to develop new skills and push the boundaries of what a tattoo is expected to look like.

As a consequence, this has led to the development of technologies to remove unwanted body art. Many studios offer laser treatment for the removal of bad tattoos or simply to lighten the tattoo before covering it with a more attractive piece of art. A tattoo is no longer forever, but its removal is painful and time-consuming. Some inks are harder to remove than others, and treatments cost more than the original tattoo, so be sure to choose your artist and tattoo wisely!

What constitutes a 'bad' tattoo is a matter of opinion, but people who have had laser treatment to remove their tattoos describe some common characteristics. Often the offending tattoo is an old one: perhaps the person had it done when he or she was young, failed to choose an artist wisely and was not sufficiently discerning about the quality of work or its subject matter, or the positioning of the tattoo on the body. Sometimes the tattoo is on a part of the body that is seldom covered – the head or hands, for example – which may cause problems in terms of interaction with others or of employability. Other 'bad' tattoos may simply be poor artwork consisting of uneven lines, colours that 'bleed' into one another, and badly proportioned images. In some instances, the tattoo may not have aged well and what started out as very intricate work now just looks messy.

I have worked in the tattoo industry for a number of years and seen trends come and go or evolve into new styles entirely.

Tattoos have become increasingly complex. Between the 1930s and the 1970s, the predominant style was that of basic two-dimensional designs depicting naval motifs, pin-ups and good-luck charms; the quality and tonal range of these tattoos were dictated by the inks and equipment available at the time. Today's artists can achieve much more sophisticated results by replicating painterly and photographic effects on people's skin.

The revival of 1950s fashions in recent years has seen a resurgence of the traditional pin-up, both as an icon and a model of beauty to which girls may aspire. Of course, at the dawn of the 21st century the pin-up is street-wise – no longer naïve and supplicating, but strong and independent. This spirit is reflected in the ubiquity of female tattoo artists, a greater number of visible tattoos on women and a wider choice of subject matter in tattoo designs.

In the 1980s and 1990s, black ink tribal work and monochrome biomechanic designs inspired by H. R. Giger's artwork were all the rage. However, now a fashion for new traditionally coloured pieces and photo-realistic tattoos has taken naval and portrait work to a different level. The earlier trends have not completely disappeared but have merely adapted to the changing sensibilities of artists and clients. These trends have evolved into a range of genres that are often blended in an organic fusion style. One of the oldest genres in the tattoo world, the Japanese style, is interpreted by countless artists even though few of them have trained with Japanese tattoo masters. But the iconography and strength of the symbols are so captivating that this has become one of the most popular types of tattoo art in the West today.

The examples of tattoo art in the following pages demonstrate the skills and techniques of the artists and the range of design ideas available to enthusiasts – from the natural world to celebrity portraits, and from elaborate dot work to symbols of the modern age.

TOP
Tattoo by Mark Gibson, Monki Do, Belper, UK.

BOTTOM LEFT
By Dawnii, Painted Lady Tattoo Parlour, Birmingham, UK.

BOTTOM CENTRE
By Sam Ricketts, Mantra Tattoo Studio, Cheltenham, UK.

BOTTOM RIGHT
Highly stylized Maori work by Lionel, Johnny Two Thumb Tattoo Studio, Singapore.

PURE DESIGN

The images included here show highly stylized tattoos. The artists who have created them use lines and shapes and often even just simple dots to produce striking designs. They combine small abstract motifs to achieve wonderfully subtle patterns and figures or take pictorial elements and break them down to their fundamental components, which they then tattoo onto the client in individual abstract patterns. Sometimes a pictorial tattoo is surrounded by abstract patterns to elevate it and make it stand out. Somewhat surprisingly, this type of work is not a new development; it has grown out of hundreds of years of tattoo practice and has become more stylized and sophisticated over the centuries.

Most tattoo line and dot work has its origins in tribal designs. However, a British practitioner called Xed LeHead has almost singlehandedly developed the technique of dot work, which has spread around the world and been adopted by artists who love this deceptively simple-looking method. Tattoo designs of this kind not only look good on the skin, they are loaded with symbolic meaning. The effect is often light and airy, with plenty of natural skin left around the tattoo or in between the various elements of the work. Line and dot work is often monochrome, reinforcing its link with the tribal patterns from which it originated.

FACING PAGE: Intricate and delicate dot work machine-free tattoos by Boff Konkerz, Roadmaps for the Soul, London, UK.

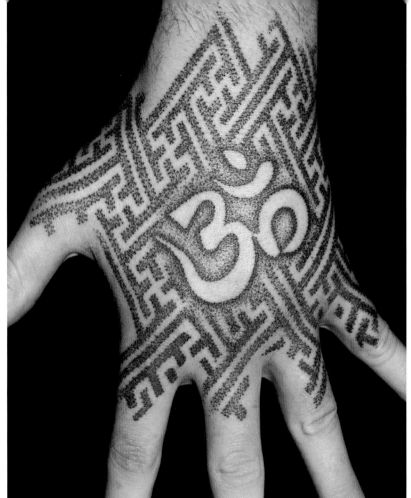

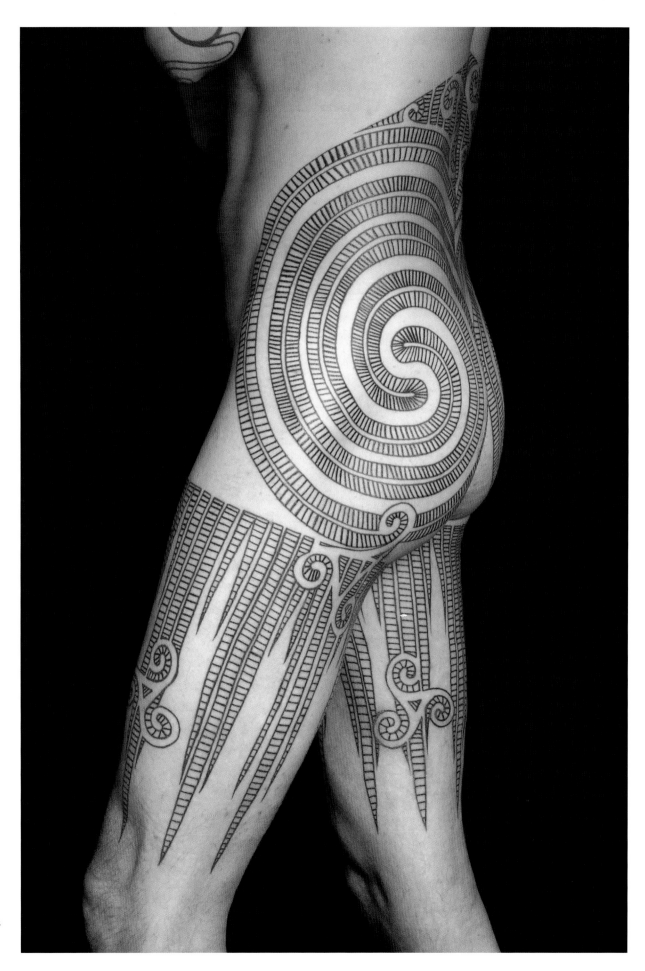

FACING PAGE:
TOP LEFT
The upper section of this tattoo is inspired by Marquesan work. Tattoo by Tiziano Ripanti of Falconara, Italy and an unknown artist in New Caledonia.

TOP RIGHT
This tattoo by Cameron Stewart consists of a striking dot-work pattern surrounding an Om symbol. Tattoo by Metalurgey, Dundee, UK.

BOTTOM LEFT
Straight out of a Dan Brown novel, this ambigram can be read both ways up. Tattoo by Mark Armstrong of Sacred Art Tattoo, Manchester, UK.

BOTTOM RIGHT
These delicate dot-work foot tattoos are machine-free designs by Boff Konkerz of Roadmaps for the Soul, London, UK.

THIS PAGE:
An intricate tribal pattern inspired by Maori art. Tattoo by Chris Bagnall of Aquaries Tattoo Studio, Cornwall, UK.

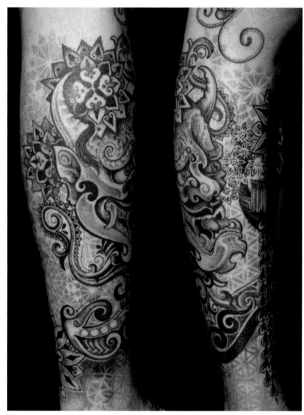

TOP AND BOTTOM LEFT
A Maori-inspired shoulder tattoo by Chris Bagnall of Aquaries Tattoo Studio, Cornwall, UK.

TOP AND BOTTOM RIGHT
A Japanese mask and geisha face are delicately interwoven with subtle abstract grey work. Although the tattoo coverage is very detailed, it is not too heavy. Tattoo by Amanda Ruby of The Jewel in the Lotus, Folkestone, UK.

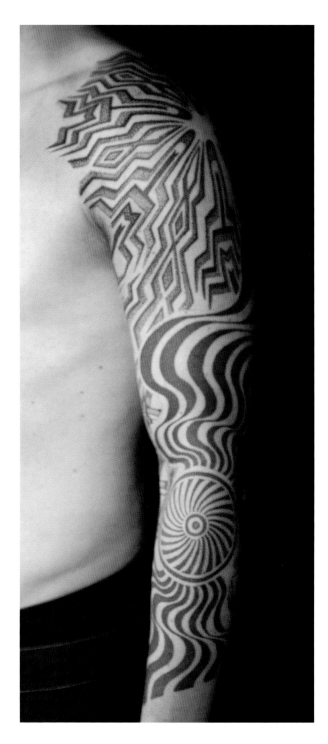

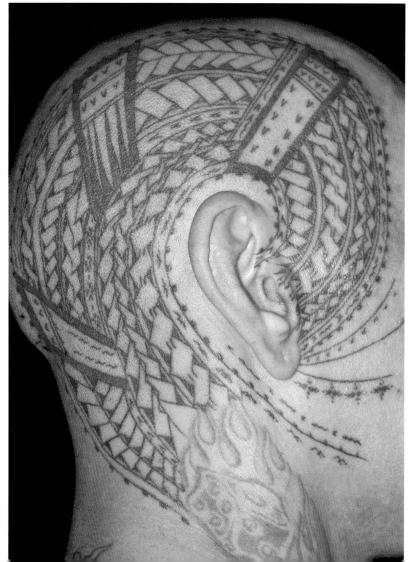

ABOVE
An optical pattern mixes different shapes and textures. Tattoo by Jannini of White Light, Berlin, Germany.

TOP RIGHT
An Aztec-inspired tattoo reproduces a deity carved in stone. Tattoo by Pavel Angel, Moscow, Russia.

BOTTOM RIGHT
A striking and intricate head tattoo by Pacific Polynesian tattoo specialist Brent McCown of Tattoo Tatau, Landskron, Austria.

THIS PAGE:
A bold Polynesian-style back piece, perfect for a large canvas. The elements on the shoulder blades are balanced by the smaller designs on the lower back. Tattoo by Jan of Für Immer, Berlin, Germany.

FACING PAGE:
TOP LEFT
An elaborate hand tattoo incorporating some dot work by Steve B of Seven Star Tattoo, Bexleyheath, UK.

TOP RIGHT
Eastern art influences this beautiful lotus flower pattern tattooed in black and grey by Avishai Tene of Ink Junkies, Luxembourg.

BOTTOM LEFT
This hand tattoo by Patrick Hüttlinger of Sakrosankt, London, UK, involves some intricate dot work.

BOTTOM RIGHT
Striking black work sets off a Borneo rosette. Tattoo by Robert Kornajzel of One More Tattoo, Luxembourg.

TOP LEFT
A back piece inspired by North American Haida artwork. Tattoo by Butch of Ultimate Skin, Leeds, UK.

TOP RIGHT
A freshly tattooed spiritual black and grey piece by Micky of Vital Element, Alicante, Spain.

BOTTOM LEFT
See page 11

BOTTOM RIGHT
A machine-free piece by Adam Sage of Into U, Brighton, UK.

TOP LEFT
A tattoo of an ancient warrior in a horned helmet framed with Celtic motifs by Steve Hunter of Touch of Ink, Portsmouth, UK.

TOP RIGHT
A bold monochrome piece by Brent McCown of Tattoo Tatau, Landskron, Austria.

BOTTOM LEFT
A Celtic tribal back piece by Spacey of Bizarre Ink, Edinburgh, UK.

BOTTOM RIGHT
The Hindu deity Ganesh has been tattooed machine-free by Boff Konkerz of Roadmaps for the Soul, London, UK.

FAMOUS FACES

The power of celebrity and popular culture means that certain iconic images are rooted in the collective unconscious. Many of the tattoos in this chapter take the form of photo-realistic portraits based on personal mementos or famous pictures. Often people choose to have tattoos of actors not so much for their off-screen personalities as for the characters they portray; or sometimes to mark a symbolic moment at which the actor's 'real' and screen images appear to elide. For example, following his untimely death, there was huge demand for tattoos of actor Heath Ledger in his last and most troubled role as the Joker in the film *The Dark Knight*.

A celebrity tattoo is often a tribute to a favourite movie or performance. Sometimes it is a memorial tattoo to a dead rock star (see the inked tributes to Amy Winehouse, Elvis Presley and John Lennon in the following pages), which serves to mark the importance their music has played and continues to play in the person's life.

Our visually over-stimulated, celebrity-obsessed society bombards us with images at every turn; whether we like it or not, these images filter into our subconscious and stay with us. It is therefore unsurprising that many people want to wear the mark of a favourite singer or actor who has moved them in some way. In the past we stuck pin-ups on our bedroom walls; now we have them tattooed on our bodies.

FACING PAGE: The gender-bending appeal of androgynous-trailblazer Marlene Dietrich is accentuated in this tattoo by Marek of Independent Tattoo, Edinburgh, UK.

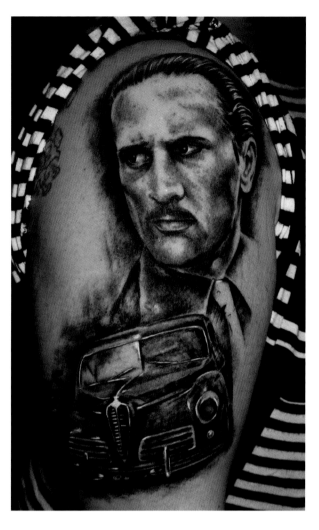

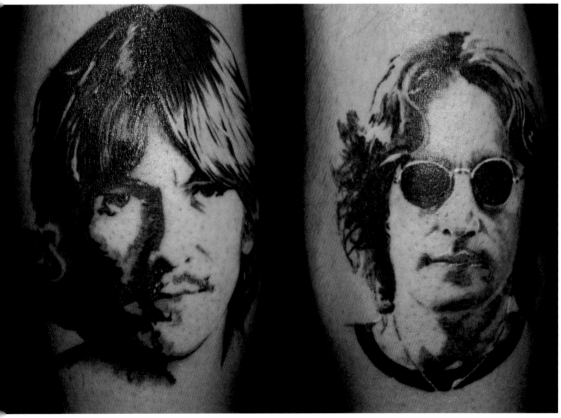

TOP LEFT
A Clint Eastwood portrait inspired by
the rugged loner he plays in many of
his movies, in this case the western
Unforgiven. Tattoo by Sissou of Insolit
Tattoo, Nîmes, France.

TOP CENTRE
Geek and musical genius Buddy Holly by
Michael Rose of Tattoo Centre, Germany.

TOP RIGHT
Robert De Niro in his career-defining role
as the young Don Vito Corleone in *The
Godfather: Part II*. Tattoo by Noellia of
Imperium Tattoo, Zaragoza, Spain.

LEFT
Loved, worshipped and missed –
Beatles members George Harrison
and John Lennon by New Road Tattoo,
Southampton, UK.

TOP LEFT
Italian marble statuary comes to life in this subtly nuanced art by Miguel Angel of V Tattoo, Aldaya, Valencia, Spain.

TOP RIGHT
Christ is often represented on skin; this haloed version is part of a large religious leg piece by José Lopez of Lowrider, California, USA.

BOTTOM LEFT
The glorious black and grey work of these leg tattoos faithfully reproduces the chiaroscuro of the originals. Tattoos by Miguel Angel of V Tattoo, Aldaya, Valencia, Spain.

BOTTOM RIGHT
A suffering Christ in a crown of thorns is sensitively rendered by Andy Engel of Andy's Tattoo, Kitzingen, Germany.

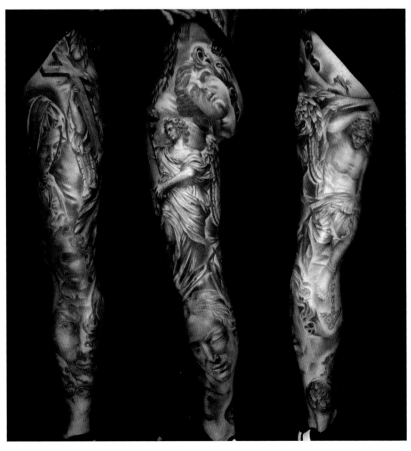

FACING PAGE:
Rock icon Gene Simmons (aka 'The Demon') of Kiss reproduced in all his grisly spectacle by photo-realism master Andy Engel of Andy's Tattoo, Kitzingen, Germany.

THIS PAGE:
TOP LEFT
Smirking, enigmatic and troubled, Heath Ledger's Joker is one of the most popular Batman bad guy tattoo subjects. Tattoo by Paul Owen of Naughty Needles, Bolton, UK.

TOP RIGHT
A glowing Amy Winehouse at the height of her success by Nikko Hurtado, Los Angeles, California, USA.

BOTTOM LEFT
Elvis mid-career in glorious Technicolor by Miss Nico of All Style Tattoo, Berlin, Germany.

BOTTOM RIGHT
A small but striking black-and-grey portrait of soul singer and pianist Ray Charles by Cristian Radu, Skinworks, Cologne, Germany.

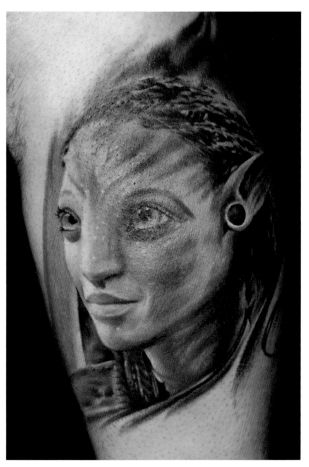

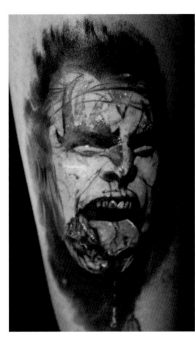

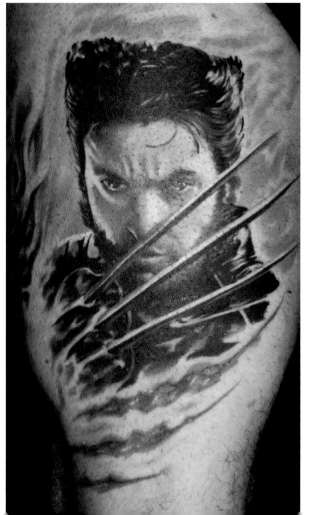

ABOVE
Ghost ship captain Davy Jones from *Pirates of the Caribbean: Dead Man's Chest*, the second instalment of the Disney movie saga. Tattoo by Steve Prizeman of Eternal Art, Chelmsford, UK.

ABOVE RIGHT
Feisty free spirit Neytiri from *Avatar*. Tattoo by Tom Sugar of Global Tattoo Studios, Moreton, UK.

BOTTOM LEFT
Even gorier than before! Gene Simmons tattoo by Javi Martin of Mao y Cathy, Madrid, Spain.

BOTTOM RIGHT
Mutant superhero Wolverine and his blades by Tom Sugar of Global Tattoo Studios, Moreton, UK.

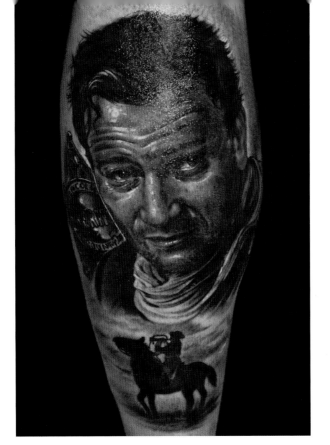

TOP LEFT
John Wayne, movie icon and star of the western genre, fittingly tattooed in black and grey by Freddy of Exotic Tattoo, Murcia, Spain.

TOP RIGHT
Enjoying the smell of napalm in the morning – Robert Duvall as Colonel Kilgore in *Apocalypse Now*. Tattoo by Xavi Garcia Boix, Tattoo Crew, Valencia, Spain.

BOTTOM LEFT
Fashion model Twiggy in her Swinging Sixties heyday. Tattoo by Leigh Oldcorn of Cosmic Tattoo, Colchester, UK.

BOTTOM RIGHT
Enduring, disturbed and disturbing – Robert De Niro as anti-hero Travis Bickle in *Taxi Driver*. Tattoo by Xavi Garcia Boix, Tattoo Crew, Valencia, Spain.

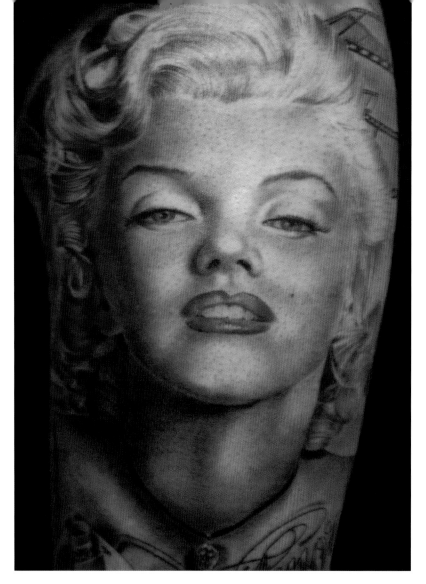

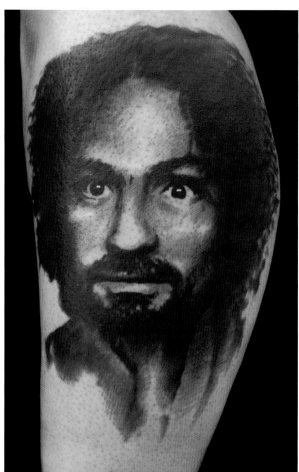

TOP LEFT
Marilyn Monroe's glamorous image is still in demand as a tattoo subject. This one is by Miguel Angel of V Tattoo, Aldaya, Valencia, Spain.

TOP RIGHT
Legendary guitarist Jimi Hendrix immortalized on skin by Andy Bowler of Monki Do, Belper, UK.

BOTTOM LEFT
Iconoclastic musician and artist Marilyn Manson is a powerfully transgressive subject in this piece by Wanted Tattoo, Barcelona, Spain.

BOTTOM RIGHT
A portrait of multiple murderer Charles Manson, minus the swastika on his forehead but still conveying the deranged look in his eyes. Tattoo by Andy Bowler of Monki Do, Belper, UK.

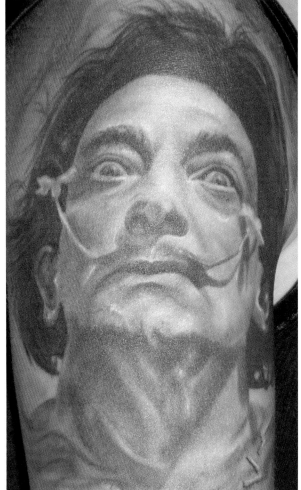

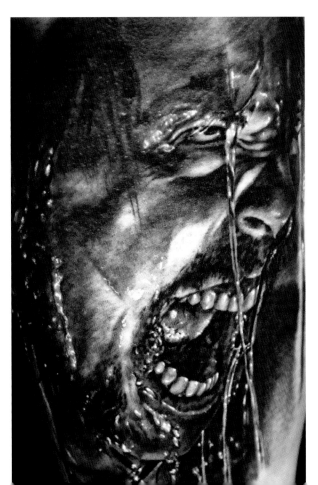

TOP LEFT
Scientific genius Albert Einstein appears alongside one of his famous statements: 'Everything should be made as simple as possible, but not simpler.' Tattoo by Daksi of Planet Tattoo, Czech Republic.

TOP RIGHT
Surrealist artist Salvador Dalí in a typically eccentric pose which emphasizes his famous waxed moustache. Tattoo by Takacs, Hungary.

BOTTOM LEFT
Portrait of James Hetfield taken from a photograph of a live Metallica gig. Tattoo by Andy Engel of Andy's Tattoo, Kitzingen, Germany.

BOTTOM RIGHT
A realistic rendition of heavy metal musician Lemmy by Andy Engel of Andy's Tattoo, Kitzingen, Germany.

FANTASY WORLD

Fantasy and horror are compelling genres that allow us to examine and process some of our wildest dreams and deepest fears. Tattoos inspired by these imaginary worlds are certainly not for the squeamish, and some people might question why anyone would want to carry such ghastly graffiti around with them at all times! But for aficionados, the horror or fantasy tattoo is the ultimate symbol of affection and affiliation, expressing a deep love for the genres and their icons. Fantasy figures from games, comics and movies are reproduced as tattoos which sometimes mix stories and characters to create a new tableau. As with realistic tattoo portraiture, the images are often taken from stills or official photographs. Occasionally the subjects are woven together in custom work to showcase the creative and interpretative skills of the tattoo artist.

The popularity of vampire movies and TV shows in recent years has led to an explosion in the horror tattoo genre. There is apparently no limit to the number of bloodcurdling creatures who can be summoned up to populate human skin! The resulting tattoos may be disturbing and scary at first glance, but their power to shock tends to fade with the years. Tattoo tributes to icons of old horror movies such as *Frankenstein* (starring Boris Karloff) or *Dracula* (starring Bela Lugosi) are inked more in loving tribute than with the expectation to revolt and terrify.

FACING PAGE: A beautiful zombie with glaucous eyes and cracked, blotchy undead skin by Andy Engel of Andy's Tattoo, Kitzingen, Germany.

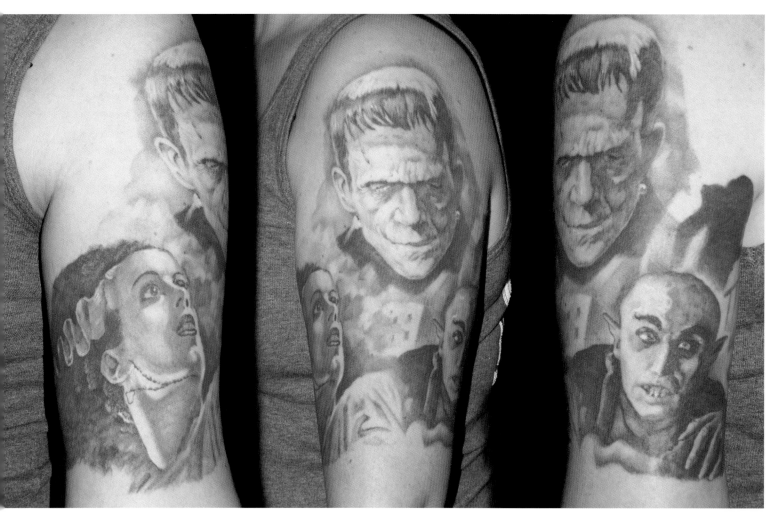

ABOVE
Homage to vintage horror movie icons the Bride of Dracula, Frankenstein and Nosferatu. Tattoos by Maze of Santa Sangre, Cologne, Germany.

BOTTOM LEFT
Another interpretation of Boris Karloff as 'Frankenstein's monster'. Tattoo by Steve Hunter of Touch of Ink, Portsmouth, UK.

BOTTOM RIGHT
Buddy Holly – but not as you know him! This zombie version is by Dero of Plus 48, Edinburgh, UK.

FACING PAGE:
TOP LEFT
A fantastical scene with a futuristic Icarus by Meehow, Cheltenham, UK.

FAR RIGHT
A portrait of a beautiful young girl with sinister undertones and a splash of blood-red colour by Robert Hernandez, Spain.

BOTTOM LEFT
The Captain Spaulding character from the film *House of 1000 Corpses*. Tattoo by Dero of Plus 48, Edinburgh, UK.

BOTTOM CENTRE
A zombie geisha mixes the macabre with exotic glamour. Tattoo by The Shining Tattoo, Huelva, Spain.

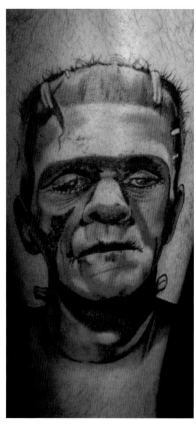

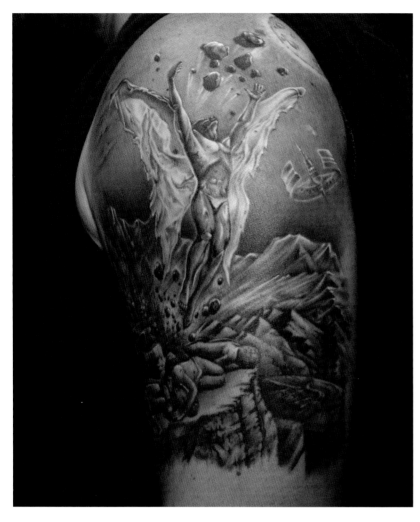

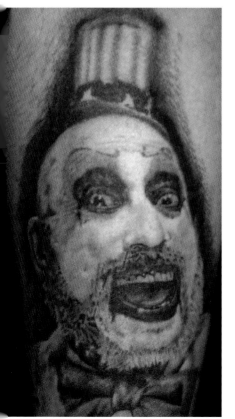

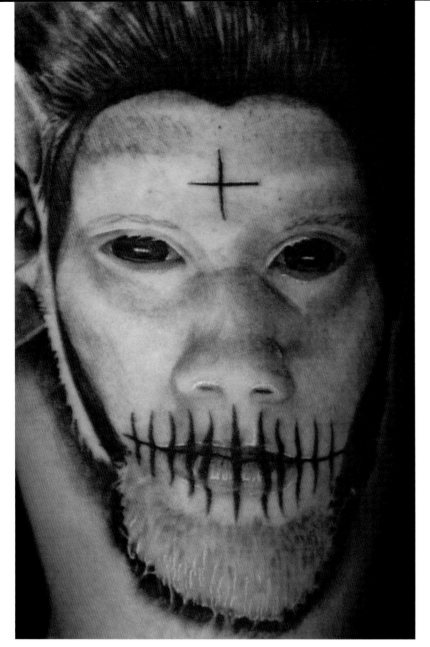

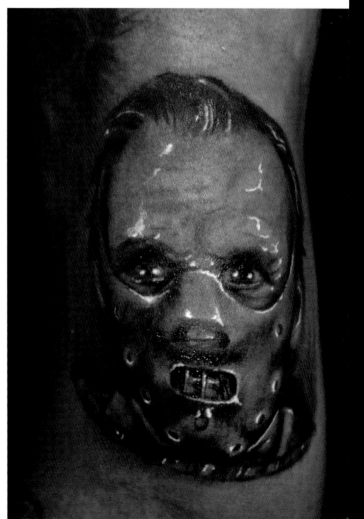

FACING PAGE:
LEFT
David Lloyd's illustrations for the *V for Vendetta* comic book series featured this iconic mask of the mysterious freedom fighter 'V'. Tattoo by George Mavridis of Tattooligans, Thessaloniki, Greece.

TOP RIGHT
Pinhead, one of the most menacing figures in modern horror, from the 1987 movie *Hellraiser*. Tattoo by Tofi of Inkognito, Rybnik, Poland.

BOTTOM RIGHT
Blending horror with comedy, this tongue-in-cheek anti-hero, Hellboy, has a well-meaning temperament. Tattoo by Ken Patten of Tattoo Station, Newcastle, UK.

THIS PAGE:
ABOVE
A black-and-grey zombie portrait by The Shining Tattoo, Huelva, Spain.

TOP RIGHT
From *A Nightmare on Elm Street*, one of horror's most successful and prolific franchises, the demonic Freddy Krueger, complete with slasher glove. Tattoo by Steve Hunter of Touch of Ink, Portsmouth, UK.

BOTTOM RIGHT
The cannibalistic Hannibal Lecter glares from this tattoo by Sean Sparks of Merlin Tattooing, Dover, UK.

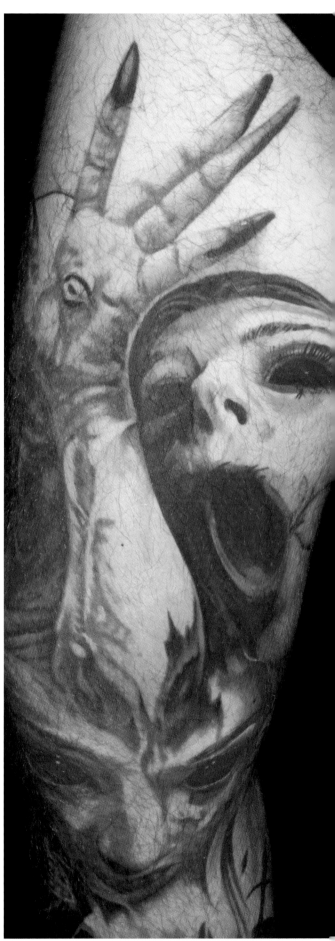

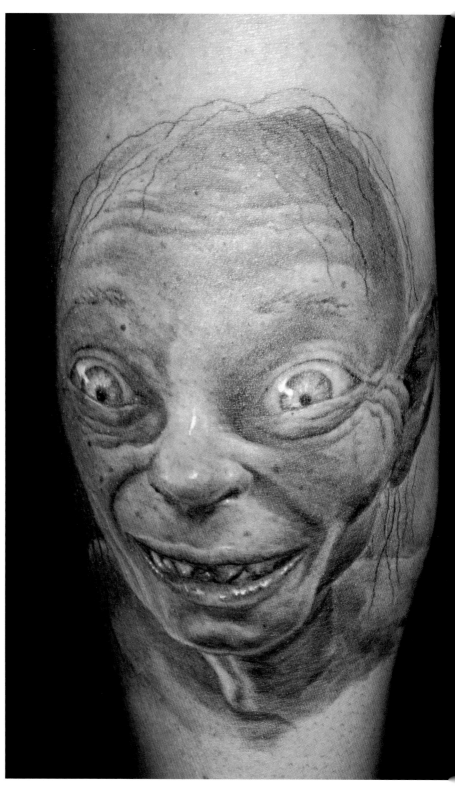

FACING PAGE:
A leg dedicated to the creatures from horror-fantasy movie *Pan's Labyrinth* and other characters. Tattoo by Mike Koren of Internal Tattoo, Bruch, Austria.

THIS PAGE:
TOP LEFT
A head tattoo which combines a demon with a Green Man, by Kevin Paul of 7th Day Tattoo, Derby, UK.

BOTTOM LEFT
A nightmarish vision in monochrome: demons and skulls by Liorcifer of Tribulation Tattoo, New York, USA.

ABOVE
The Lord of the Rings trilogy has spawned a lot of memorable characters, none creepier than the corrupted hobbit Gollum. Tattoo by Anabi, Anabi Tattoo, Szczecin, Poland.

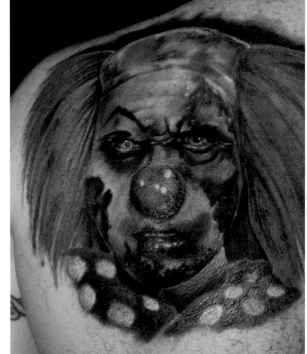

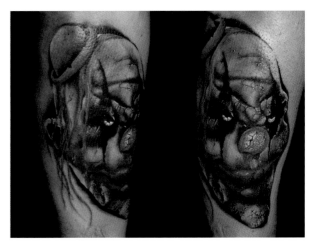

ABOVE
Long seen as tragi-comic figures, clowns have also gained a reputation as evil and sinister. Stephen King and *It* have a lot to answer for! Tattoo by Arran Burton of Cosmic Tattoo, Colchester, UK.

TOP RIGHT
The terrifying green-haired clown from *Zombieland*. Tattoo by Roy Priestley of Skinshokz, Wyke, Bradford, UK.

CENTRE RIGHT
Dishevelled and scary, this clown is inspired by Heath Ledger's Joker in *The Dark Knight*. Tattoo by Roy Priestley of Skin Shokz, Wyke, Bradford, UK.

BOTTOM RIGHT
Almost ghostly, this clown tattoo with butterflies is striking for its use of black, grey and red inks. Tattoo by Leigh Oldcorn of Cosmic Tattoo, Colchester, UK.

FACING PAGE:
Creepy and unsettling, with more than a passing resemblance to the Aphex Twin portrait. Tattoo by Andy Engel of Andy's Tattoo, Kitzingen, Germany.

FACING PAGE:
TOP LEFT
With mascara running down her face and a terrified expression, this girl looks as though she has seen a ghost – or worse! Tattoo by Magda Zon of 13 Diamonds, London, UK.

TOP RIGHT
Sexy female zombie by Scott Irwin, aka Coolaid, of One More Tattoo, Luxembourg.

BOTTOM LEFT AND RIGHT
A sleeve dedicated to vampires from different movies. Tattoos by Csaba Muellner of Modification, Germany.

THIS PAGE:
LEFT
A zombie beauty in unnatural colours, bandaged in crime scene tape. Tattoo by Mason of Poison Ink, Basingstoke, UK.

BOTTOM LEFT
A horned devil tattooed in black and brown by David Hernandez of Modern Angels, Talavera, Spain.

BOTTOM CENTRE
A striking mutant sex kitten bathed in moonlight by Dan Banas of Bananas Tattoo, Formby, UK.

BOTTOM RIGHT
A sugar skull girl and other images of mortality by Kamil of Kamil Tattoos, London, UK.

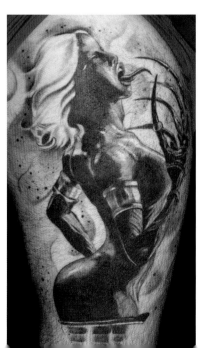

NATURAL WORLD

Feeling at one with nature is a state to which many people aspire. It represents a return to simpler times, a desire to experience the environment at a primal level and a wish to elevate ourselves spiritually. Human actions alter the natural world inexorably and many of us believe that we plunder the environment without much concern for the future. A tattoo of things we find in nature is a tribute to something we love, something we long for and something we believe we may have lost.

Tattoos of the natural world tend to be animal portraits or flowers rather than general scenery, although the great outdoors often features in large pieces as a background. Animals are an obvious choice for the tattoo lover who wants a lasting memento of a lost pet or seeks empowerment through a totemic animal whose energy can be channelled to gain enlightenment and insight. Some ancient tribes (and Native Americans to this day) believed that every human was born with an animal spirit guide (the word 'animal' derives from the Latin 'anima', meaning soul) from which wisdom and power could be gained.

Plants, especially flowers, lend themselves particularly well to tattoos as they are intricate and can be reproduced organically, creating movement in the art. Of course they are also very beautiful and colourful, often appearing as decorative elements (with specific meanings) on bigger images – for example, cherry blossom or lotus flowers in Eastern-inspired tattoos.

FACING PAGE: A dynamic portrait of a galloping horse in black and grey adorns a woman's back. Tattoo by Derek Young of Yankee Tattoos, Dundee, UK.

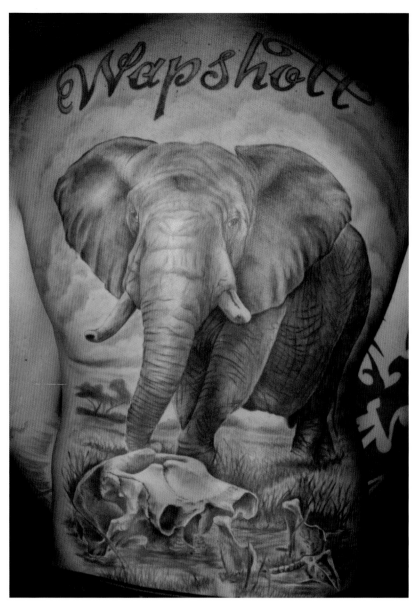

TOP LEFT
Colourful and striking, this tiger is so animated it looks as though it's about to jump off the skin! Tattoo by Irene Thill of One More Tattoo, Luxembourg.

TOP RIGHT
A black-and-grey back piece highlights the plight of elephants and their slaughter for the ivory trade. Tattoo by Alie K, Toronto, Canada.

BOTTOM LEFT
A photo-realistic, powerful lion portrait by Dani Martos of Demon Tattoo, Lerida, Spain.

LEFT
This shoulder portrait of a primate has an air of melancholy. Tattoo by Jin, Jin Tattoo, Oxford, UK.

TOP LEFT
A tiger peers through leaves (shown as cutouts of naked skin) in the undergrowth. Tattoo by J Cuba of New Ethnic Tattoo, Moscow, Russia.

TOP RIGHT
A tiger with white stripes dominates this Japanese-style tattoo by Richie Clarke of Tribal Life, Liverpool, UK.

BOTTOM LEFT
A stunning back and legs tattoo depicts a tiger in shades of blue, by Colin Jones of Stained Class Tattoo, Shrewsbury, UK.

RIGHT
Endangered species: a leopard peers from this striking back piece by Chikai, Russia.

THIS PAGE:
TOP LEFT
Tropical sea life makes up this beautiful leg piece by Miss Nico of All Style Tattoo, Berlin, Germany.

TOP RIGHT
An underwater scene in glorious marine colours by Miss Nico of All Style Tattoo, Berlin, Germany.

BOTTOM LEFT
A large carp swims upstream in this strong back piece by Derek Campbell of Ultimate Tattoo, Bournemouth, UK.

BOTTOM RIGHT
Beautiful koi carps in a dark water habitat by Teresa Gordon-Wade of Lifetime Tattoo Studio, Derby, UK.

FACING PAGE:
TOP LEFT
A Japanese-style carp, a popular tattoo motif, by Rob Ratcliffe of Border Rose Tattoo Studio, Littleborough, Greater Manchester, UK.

CENTRE
Cartoon-like, endearing fish by Irene Thill of One More Tattoo, Luxembourg.

BOTTOM
A koi carp by Aaron Hewitt of Cult Classic Tattoo, Romford, UK.

FAR RIGHT
Flowers, water and a colourful carp create a flowing movement. Tattoo by Tiba, Tiba Tattoo Studio, Berlin, Germany.

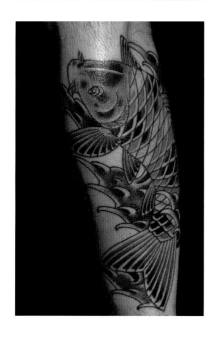

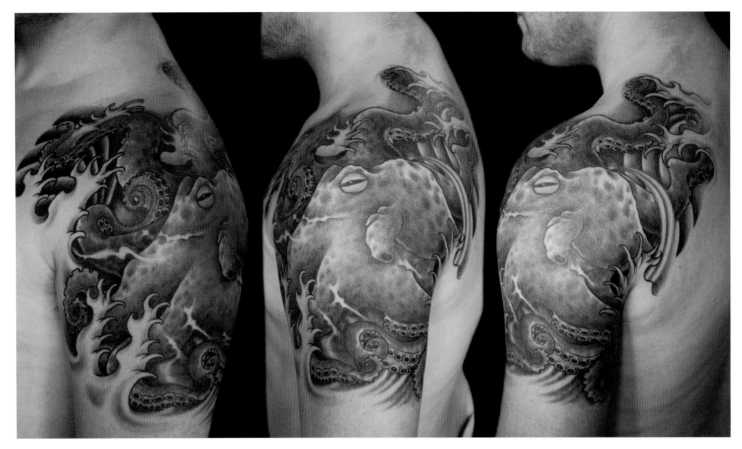

ABOVE
Wrapped around a man's shoulder, this octopus tattoo makes the most of the animal's flexible and fluid characteristics. Tattoo by Jan of Für Immer, Berlin, Germany.

FAR LEFT
A red and white koi carp with a lotus flower in flowing water, by Paul Saunders of Voodoo Tattoo, Warrington, UK.

CENTRE
A bright, colourful and cute natural scene by Endré Szabo of Tattooend, London, UK.

LEFT
A quirky, unusual frog tattoo by Jarek Slezak of Asgard, Southampton, UK.

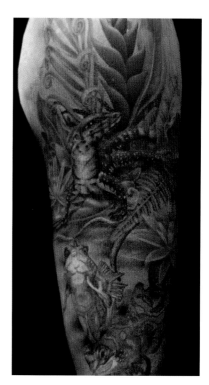

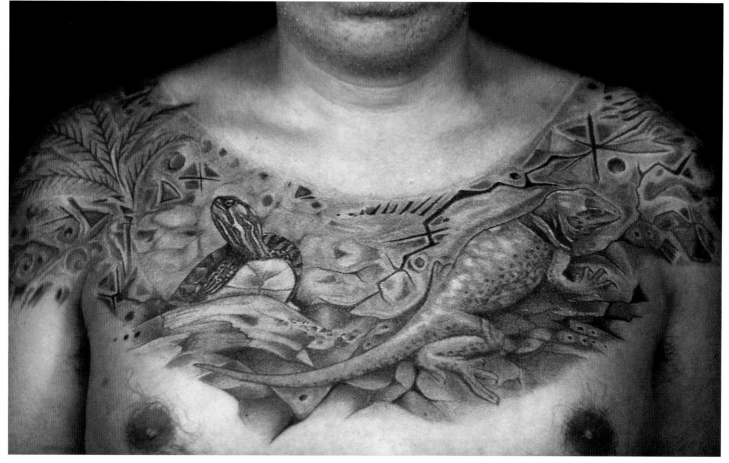

TOP LEFT
A tortoise is the centrepiece of this tattoo, full of minute details and striking design ideas. Tattoo by Avishai Tene of Ink Junkies, Luxembourg.

TOP CENTRE
Rats and a half-eaten snake are among the disturbing elements that make up this striking tattoo by Eugene of Tattooz by Design, Shirley, Southampton, UK.

TOP RIGHT
A colourful and exotic shoulder piece by Miss Nico of All Style Tattoo, Berlin, Germany.

ABOVE
A naturalistic reptilian scene against a Cubist-inspired background by Florence Amblard, Galérie d'Art, Paris, France.

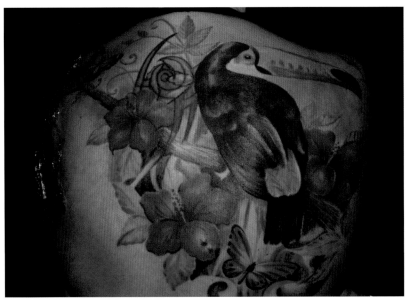

TOP LEFT
A mother penguin with her baby, by ABH, Scunthorpe, UK.

TOP RIGHT
A piece that evokes the toucan's lush tropical habitat. Tattoo by Caspar, Southampton, UK.

ABOVE
A kingfisher in mid-flight after diving for fish, by Miss Nico of All Style Tattoo, Berlin, Germany.

LEFT
A goldfinch by Mirek Vel Stotker of Stotker Tattoo, London, UK.

RIGHT
Splashes of colour and bright flowers set off this black and grey bird. Tattoo by Tony B.

FAR RIGHT
A cartoon interpretation of a bluebird, by Yliana Paolini of One More Tattoo, Luxembourg.

BELOW
Longstanding symbols of strength, power and freedom, the eagles in this tattoo are depicted in photo-realistic detail. Tattoo by Tom Sugar of Global Tattoo Studios, Moreton, UK.

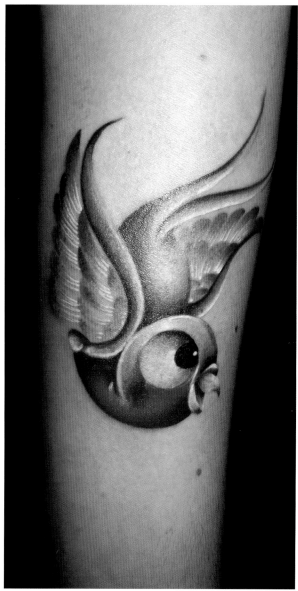

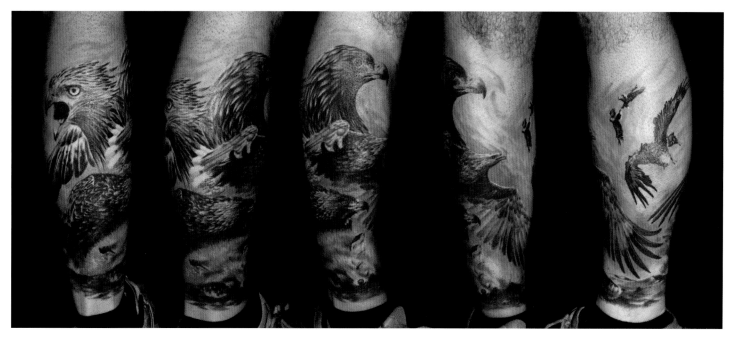

TOP LEFT
Noon's distinctive artistic style ensures that these quirky dragonflies grab the attention. Tattoo by Noon of Boucherie Traditionnelle, France.

TOP RIGHT
The delicate, almost tactile treatment of the butterflies' wings gives this tattoo a 3D effect. Tattoo by Yliana Paolini of One More Tattoo, Luxembourg.

BOTTOM LEFT
Full of movement, this dragonfly tattoo has a strong visual impact. Tattoo by Leslie Reesen of Mad Science, The Hague, Netherlands.

BOTTOM RIGHT
A hummingbird feeds from a flower with a metallic heart in this tattoo by Niewczas, Czas Tattoo, Leicester, UK.

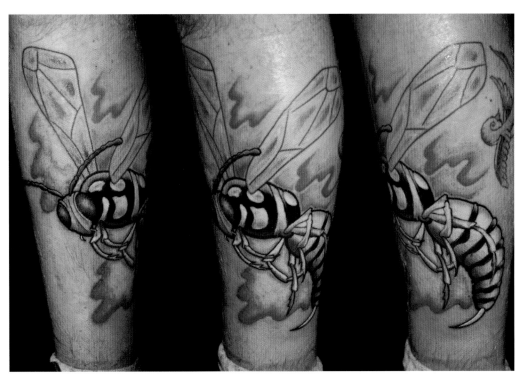

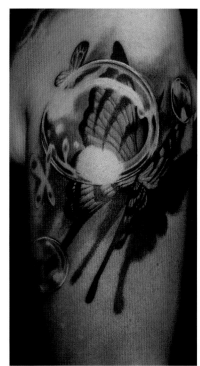

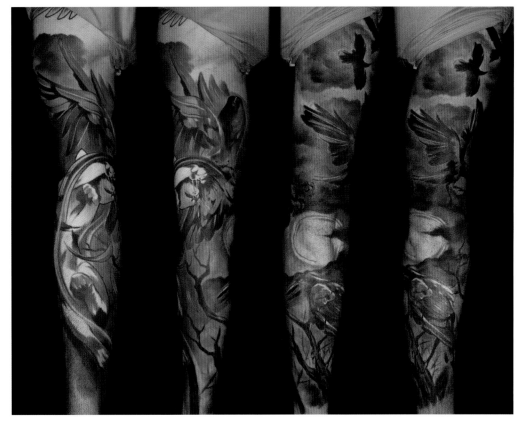

TOP LEFT
A giant wasp with a terrifying sting in this bold tattoo by Aaron Millett, Portsmouth, UK.

TOP RIGHT
A butterfly seen through a bubble, with a shadow that gives this image depth. Tattoo by Victor Policheri, VIP Tattoo, Barcelona, Spain.

BOTTOM LEFT
A dragonfly, a butterfly, limpid colours and movement. Tattoo by Andy Bowler of Monki Do, Belper, UK.

BOTTOM RIGHT
A dynamic, bold, painterly natural scene by Kamil of Kamil Tattoos, London, UK.

TOP LEFT
A strikingly drawn bunch of multicoloured roses with strong black contour lines. Roses by Scott Commons and ladybird by Máximo Lutz of Blood & Tears Tattoo, Barcelona, Spain.

TOP RIGHT
Bold design and vivid colours distinguish this beautiful lotus flower tattoo by Magda Zon of 13 Diamonds, London, UK.

BOTTOM LEFT
Contoured in black, these pink hibiscus flowers make a bold statement. Tattoo by Ilona of Angelic Hell, West Worthing, UK.

BOTTOM RIGHT
This poppy and cornflower tattoo is light and feminine. Tattoo by Yliana Paolini of One More Tattoo, Luxembourg.

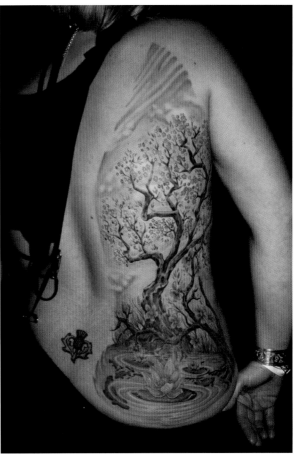

TOP LEFT
This huge daisy is crafted to great 3D effect. Tattoo by Mark Gibson of Monki Do, Belper, UK.

TOP RIGHT
Cherry blossom and lotus flowers lend this tattoo a distinctive Japanese feel. Tattoo by Tommi of No Regrets, Cheltenham, UK.

BOTTOM LEFT
Detailed, painterly poppies by Ben English of English's Electric Tattoo, Lewes, UK.

BOTTOM RIGHT
Colourful flowers follow the muscle lines of the arm in this tattoo by Magda Zon of 13 Diamonds, London, UK.

TOP LEFT
The free style of the surrounding flowers contrasts effectively with the photo-realistic, careful treatment of the two small dogs. Tattoo by Anabi, Anabi Tattoo, Szczecin, Poland.

TOP RIGHT (BOTH)
Two dogs depicted in loving detail by Andy Engel of Andy's Tattoo, Kitzingen, Germany.

RIGHT
A monochrome dog with red feathered-effect background by Steve A of Indelible Tattoo Studio, Bournemouth, UK.

FACING PAGE:
TOP LEFT
A photo-realistic portrait of an eagle by Andy Engel of Andy's Tattoo, Kitzingen, Germany.

RIGHT
A ginger kitten sitting in flowers against a monochrome background by Sister Sammy of Fallen Angel, Liverpool, UK.

BOTTOM LEFT
A cute hamster looks up expectantly. Tattoo by Scott Irwin, aka Coolaid, of One More Tattoo, Luxembourg.

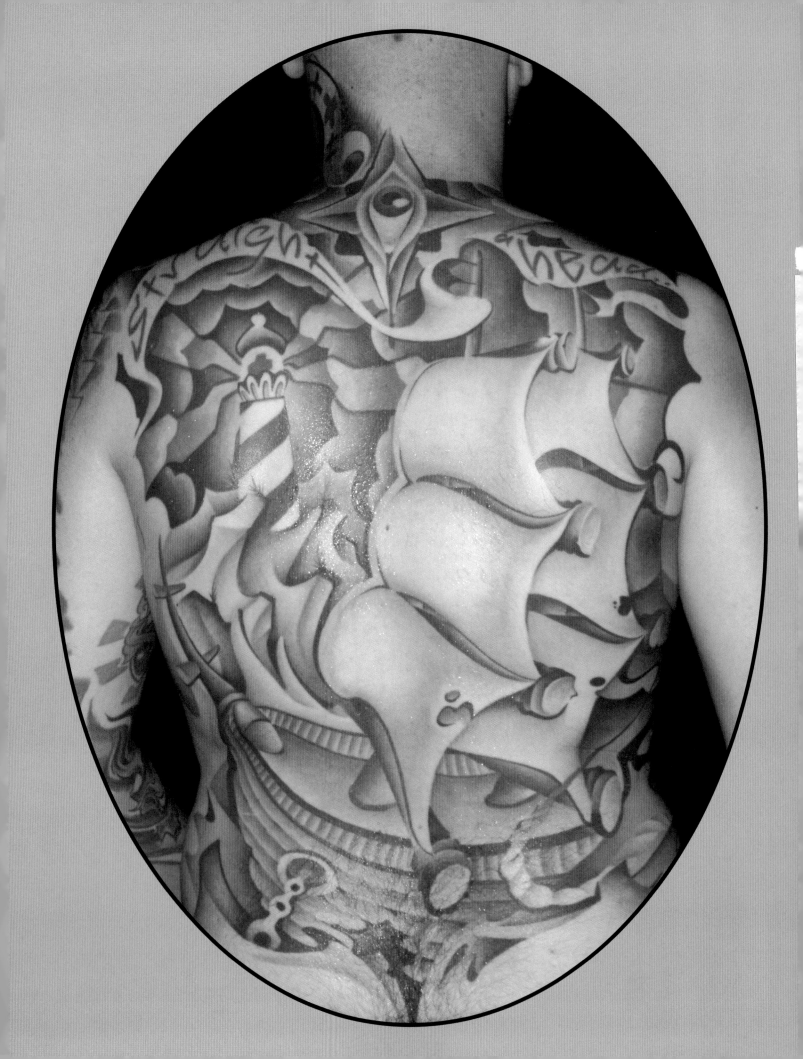

GETTING AWAY

Nautical motifs such as ships, anchors, lighthouses and compasses were among the earliest subjects for tattoos, as sailors brought them home from the South Seas to Europe and North America. For this reason, the first tattoo parlours appeared around ports and harbours. Nautical tattoos became popular following the Second World War, when naval servicemen used them to celebrate their homecoming. At the end of his tour of duty, a sailor would get a ship tattooed on his body to celebrate the achievement; the practice marked a rite of passage, a coming of age. Some sailors also regarded the tattoo as a talisman which would protect the wearer when he was away at sea.

Today, anchors, lighthouses, compasses and nautical stars are still popular as tattoo subjects, symbolizing safety, stability in the face of adversity and clarity of direction. However, in general, ship tattoos now owe less to the completion of a tour of naval duty and more to a fascination with pirates as an archetype of the free spirit in search of adventure.

Another popular transportation motif is the car, which underlines a passion for independence and travelling. For some, a car tattoo indicates nothing more than the fact that the wearer is a petrol head! But others may choose car tattoos to symbolize departure, escape and the freedom of travel and discovery.

FACING PAGE: In this deep-focus back piece, the ship in the foreground is guided by the flashing lighthouse in the distance. The compass at the top of the art incorporates an all-seeing eye. Tattoo by Ulrich Krammer of Face the Fact, Nürnberg, Germany.

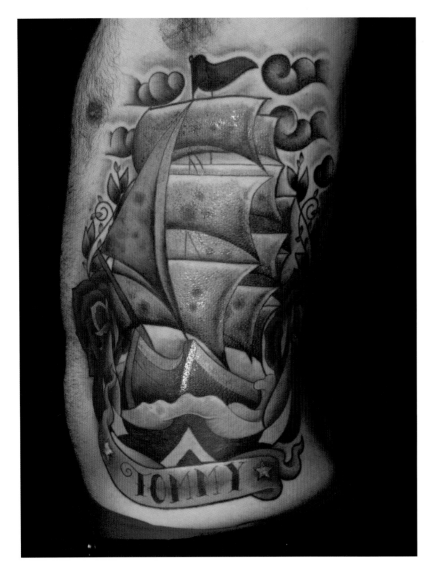

TOP LEFT
A coloured ship sails through an ocean storm. Tattoo by Leah Moule of Spear Studio, Birmingham, UK.

TOP RIGHT
A lighthouse in vivid painterly style by Tofi of Inkognito, Poland.

BOTTOM LEFT
The nautical star is often interpreted as a symbol of guidance in life. Tattoo by Jessi Manchester of All Style Tattoo, Berlin, Germany.

BOTTOM RIGHT
A monochrome ship sailing on rough seas by Jan of Für Immer, Berlin, Germany.

FACING PAGE:
In this tribute to traditional maritime tattoos, a sailing ship is framed by treacherous mermaids, a Jolly Roger, a nautical star and a sea monster. Black-and-grey tattoo by Stevie Willet, My Last One Tattoo, Portsmouth, UK.

THIS PAGE:
ABOVE
The nautical star symbolizes stability and clarity. Tattoo
by Mark Gibson of Monki Do, Belper, UK.

LEFT, TOP TO BOTTOM
Three representations of vessels at sea.
TOP: by Tom Hayball of Tattoo Monkey, Southampton, UK.
CENTRE: by Emily Hansen of World of Tattoos, Ruislip Manor, UK.
BOTTOM: an unusual monochrome sailing ship achieved using
dot work and a hand-crafted tool, by Boff Konkerz of Roadmaps
for the Soul, London, UK.

FACING PAGE:
TOP
A vintage car with brightly coloured headlights, by Neil Anderson
of abody Tattoo, Leicester, UK.

BOTTOM
Symbol of a city: the Golden Gate Bridge in San Francisco, by
Anabi of Anabi Tattoo, Szczecin, Poland.

FACING PAGE:
TOP LEFT
A fighter plane in the Land of the Rising Sun, by Mark Le Shark of 13 Ink, Liverpool, UK.

TOP RIGHT
This bike owner wears his wheels on his arm. Tattoo by Moro Tattoo of Genoa, Italy.

CENTRE RIGHT
A classic car tattoo by Gas Tattoo of Seville, Spain.

BOTTOM LEFT
An affectionate tribute to a beloved car. Tattoo by Magda Zon of 13 Diamonds, London, UK.

BOTTOM RIGHT
Car tattoo and licence plates by Jessi Manchester of All Style Tattoo, Berlin, Germany.

THIS PAGE:
A nostalgic tattoo of a vintage Volkswagen Beetle by Mario, Vienna, Austria.

LOVE OBJECTS

There is no more permanent way of showing your love than to have the object of your affection inked onto your skin. Such tattoo tokens of adoration and faith are still popular today even though, given the transience of many romantic attachments, they may not always seem a good idea. Although the love heart emblazoned with the partner's name has evolved into a more sophisticated form of tattoo art, many traditional elements remain.

Tattoo tributes include in memoriam images and even photo-realistic portraits of relatives, friends and lovers. Sometimes the tattoo symbolizes how we feel – a faithful heart, for example – but birds, pin-up girls and flowers are also popular. Once pin-ups were mementos that sailors carried around to remind them of their sweethearts back home. But today the variety of pin-ups is vast, ranging from the basic sailor girl to more elaborate reproductions of original 1950s classic pin-up artworks and comic-book heroines.

A motif that has become popular in recent times is the sugar-skull girl. This tattoo morphs Mexican Day of the Dead sugar skull decorations with the image of a pretty girl's face. Love objects don't have to be human, of course. Pets and material possessions also crop up as objects of the tattoo wearer's ardour.

FACING PAGE: Love and death in a bold tableau – a praying sugar-skull girl framed by guns and skulls. Tattoo by Leo of Naked Trust, Salzburg, Austria.

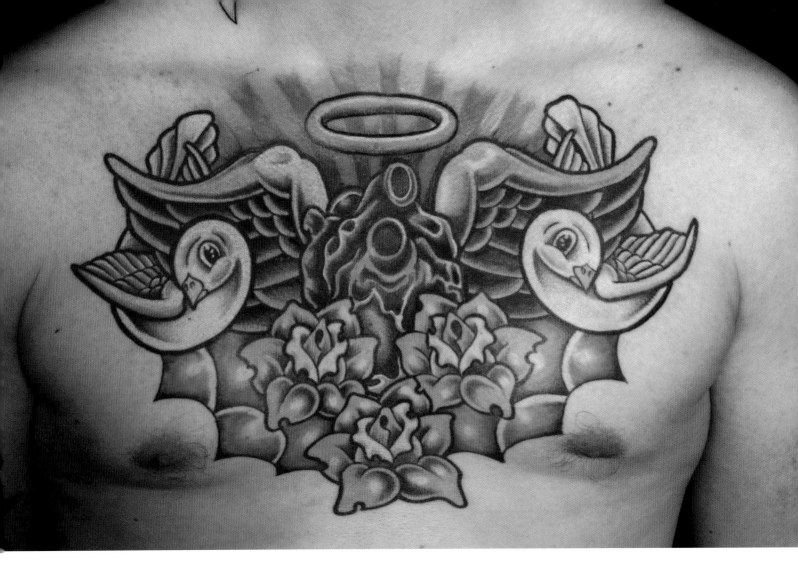

FACING PAGE:
TOP
A winged, haloed heart in physiological detail, surrounded by cartoon birds and flowers. Tattoo by Jori of The Studio, Manchester, UK.

BOTTOM
Three versions of the sugar-skull girl – unsettling images of beauty in death.

LEFT
Tattoo by George Mavridis of Tattooligans, Thessaloniki, Greece.

CENTRE
Colourful tattoo by Alessio of True Love Tattoo, London, UK.

RIGHT
The skull beneath the skin by Nikko Hurtado, Los Angeles, California, USA.

THIS PAGE:
Four more fine examples of melancholic sugar-skull girls.

TOP LEFT
Colour and movement in a tattoo by Jesus of Loyal Tattoo & Co, Murcia, Spain.

TOP RIGHT
Exotic updo hairstyle by Anabi of Anabi Tattoo, Szczecin, Poland.

BOTTOM LEFT
A monochrome version by Eric Marcinizyn, Delaware, USA.

BOTTOM RIGHT
Elfin sugar-skull girl by Angel Lopez, The Shining Tattoo, Huelva, Spain.

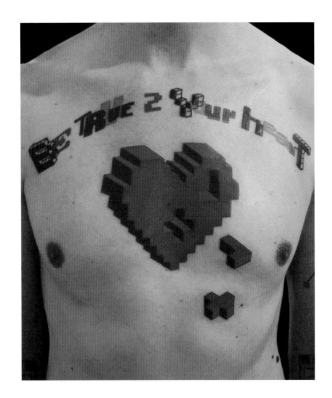

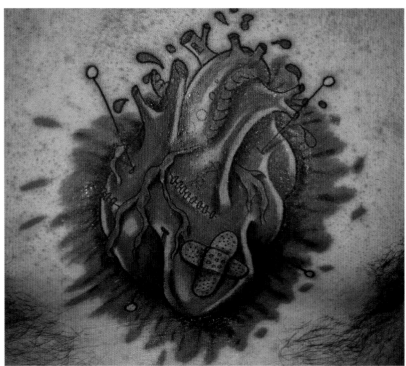

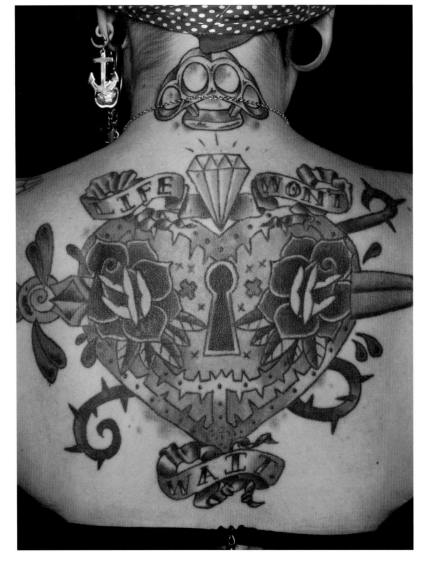

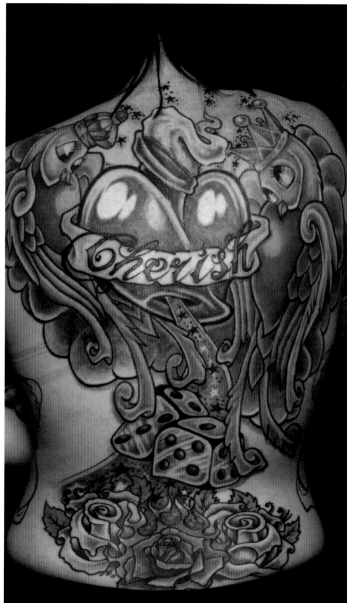

FACING PAGE:

TOP LEFT
Interesting lettering and a pixellated heart by Jef Palumbo of Boucherie Moderne, Brussels, Belgium.

TOP RIGHT
A bleeding heart with pins, scars and a sticking plaster – a symbol of recovery and survival, perhaps? Tattoo by Carlos of Kaeru Tattoo, Valencia, Spain.

BOTTOM LEFT
'Life won't wait' is the motto around this heart pierced by a sword and thorns. Back tattoo by Steve Byrne of Rock of Ages Tattoo, Austin, Texas; knuckleduster on neck by Billy Hay of Custom Inc, Glasgow, UK.

BOTTOM RIGHT
A winged heart, bleeding and decorated with traditional motifs, by Cal Fletcher of Flecky's Tattoo Studio, Wigan, UK.

THIS PAGE:

TOP LEFT
A pretty bird surrounded with symbols for a lucky love life. Tattoo by Jo Harrison of Modern Body Art, Birmingham, UK.

TOP RIGHT
A sugar-skull girl and a smoking gun: symbols of a crime of passion? Tattoo by Ronnie Goddard, Boston, Lincolnshire, UK.

ABOVE
A compass is the focal point of this black-and-grey chest piece by Jack of Evolution, Kidlington, UK.

RIGHT
A bright, colourful back piece with bluebirds, hearts, flowers and lucky dice – tokens of romantic love. Tattoo by Adam Harris of New Tribe, Brixham, Devon, UK.

THIS PAGE:

TOP LEFT
Pin-up portrait from an original illustration by Gil Elvgren. Tattoo by Andy Bowler of Monki Do, Belper, UK.

BOTTOM LEFT
Another tattoo from a classic Elvgren pin-up, by Damon Conklin of Supergenius Tattoo, Seattle, Washington, USA.

ABOVE
An unusually large, bold and colourful retro pin-up covering the whole back. Tattoo by Noi Siamese of 1969 Tattoo, Oslo, Norway.

FACING PAGE:

TOP LEFT
A corseted girl in suspenders sits on an oversized anchor. No prizes for guessing the symbolism! Tattoo by Leo of Naked Trust, Salzburg, Austria.

TOP RIGHT
A trio of lookalikes beautifully shaded in black and grey by Miguel Angel of V Tattoo, Aldaya, Valencia, Spain.

BOTTOM LEFT
A sad expression and sugar-skull markings in this portrait by Miguel Angel of V Tattoo, Aldaya, Valencia, Spain.

BOTTOM RIGHT
This Eve in the Garden of Eden is reminiscent of a manga girl. Tattoo by Leo of Naked Trust, Salzburg, Austria.

THIS PAGE:
TOP LEFT
An erotic fantasy figure for 21st-century pirate lovers. Tattoo by Vampiro Tattoo, Argentina, Brazil.

TOP RIGHT
The bold lighting echoes that of the original still from the film *Sin City*. Tattoo by Jessi Manchester of All Style Tattoo, Berlin, Germany.

BOTTOM LEFT
A photo-realistic portrait by Miguel Angel Bohigues of V Tattoo, Valencia, Spain.

BOTTOM RIGHT
Dreamy tattoo with psychedelic colouring by Tom Sugar of Global Tattoo Studios, Moreton, UK.

FACING PAGE:
TOP LEFT
A bold use of colour for this modern pin-up by Matt Lapping of Creative Vandals, Hull, UK.

TOP RIGHT
Pale colours and manga style in this kitten tattoo by Sebo of Mystery Touch, Gleisdorf, Austria.

BOTTOM LEFT
A portrait of 1950s pin-up girl Bettie Page shows off her trademark hairstyle. Tattoo by Benjamin of Tom's Tattoo World, Graz, Austria.

BOTTOM RIGHT
From an original artwork by Rachael Huntington. Tattoo by Roy Priestley of Skinshokz, Wyke, Bradford, UK.

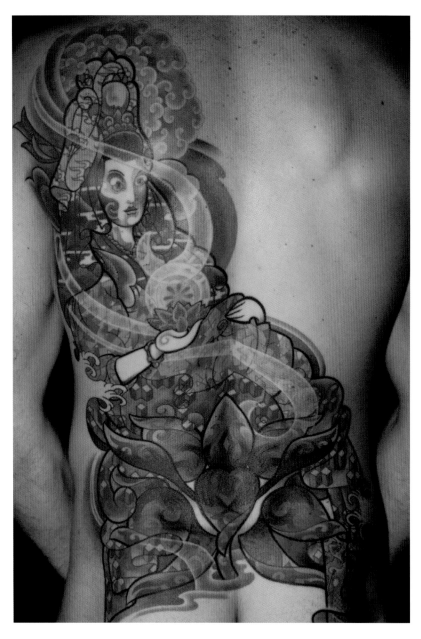

THIS PAGE:

LEFT
A stunning piece using perfectly balanced colours and Eastern motifs. Tattoo by Avishai Tene of Ink Junkies, Luxembourg.

BOTTOM LEFT
A subtly nuanced tattoo by Paolo Acuna of Divinity Tattoo, Phoenix, Arizona, USA.

BOTTOM CENTRE
Delicate colours and graceful tattoo work give this subject an ethereal quality. Tattoo by Claire Reid.

BOTTOM RIGHT
Religious symbols and bold colours for a haloed figure by Dawnii of Painted Lady Tattoo Parlour, Birmingham, UK.

FACING PAGE:
TOP LEFT
A Japanese-style girl tattooed in great detail by Leo of Naked Trust, Salzburg, Austria.

TOP RIGHT
A manga-influenced geisha rendered with decisive marks, detailed patterns and shading by Noon of Boucherie Traditionnelle, France.

BOTTOM LEFT
Vivid colours give this machine-tattooed back piece a painterly quality. Tattoo by Leo of Naked Trust, Salzburg, Austria.

BOTTOM RIGHT
A masterfully executed black-and-grey tribute to the traditional Kyoto geisha by Robert Kornajzel of One More Tattoo, Luxembourg.

THIS PAGE:
ABOVE LEFT
A cartoon girl mixes the sacred and the profane. Tattoo by Paul Reynolds of Made in Manchester, UK.

ABOVE RIGHT
Cartoon love-bunny tattoo by Paul Reynolds of Made in Manchester, UK.

FACING PAGE:
TOP
Tattoo exuding musical passion and a sense of freedom by Sean Sparks of Merlin Tattooing, Dover, UK.

BOTTOM LEFT
The heart is a popular chest tattoo. This anatomically detailed version, with its soaring wings, makes a very strong statement. Tattoo by Tanya Buxton of Monki Do, Belper, UK.

BOTTOM RIGHT
Love and music often go hand in hand. Tattooed with strong, warm colours by Anton Oleksenko of D3XS Orchestra, Gliwice, Poland.

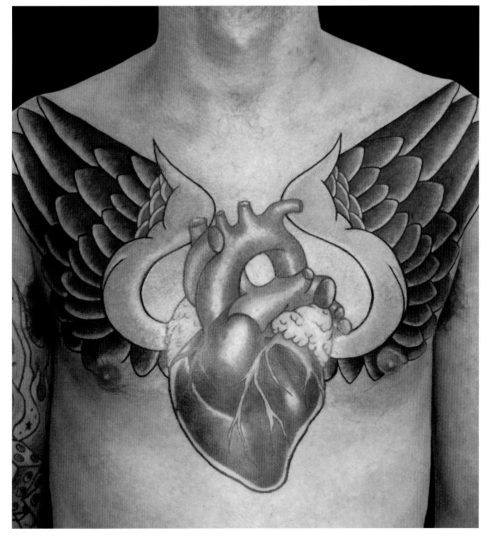

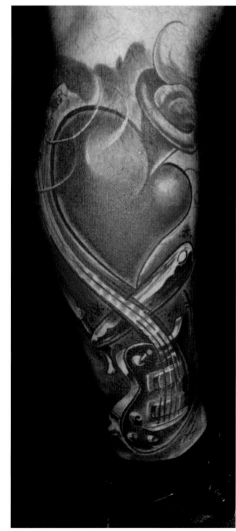

THE LIGHTER SIDE

Sometimes a tattoo is chosen just to bring a smile to our face. Humour and a nostalgic affection for the characters who populate our childhood memories have a significant influence on tattoo art. One reason for this could be that cute, funny, fluffy images simply put us in a good mood. This is why some people are happy to have visual puns or playful images inked forever on their skin. They can glance at these cartoons and humorous subjects daily to lift their spirits.

Artists such as Fabio Moro use witty concepts and crayoning techniques to convey a quirky view of life. Others, such as the French artist Noon, embrace a purity of line which gives their artwork a distinctive desaturated look. These high-impact images rely on clean lines and geometric patterns to achieve a decisive, minimalist effect. One of the brightest stars on the UK scene is artist Leah Moule, who reinterprets traditional tattoo subjects by deploying her own dazzling colours and a Disney–manga sensibility to create a strong signature style.

In general, tongue-in-cheek tattoo subjects are based on familiar images in the public domain or supplied by the client. They are then filtered through the artists' personal vision, which gives the tattoos their idiosyncratic look and mood.

FACING PAGE: The subtle yet vivid shading of this arachnophobic elephant makes it stand out against the wearer's pale skin. Tattoo by Scott Irwin, aka Coolaid, of One More Tattoo, Luxembourg.

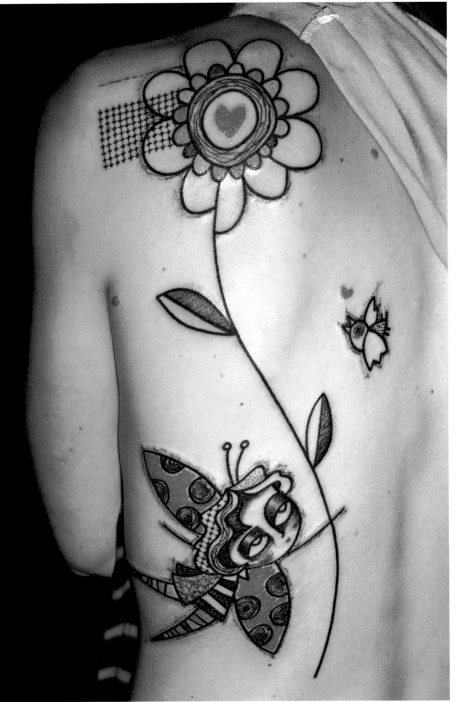

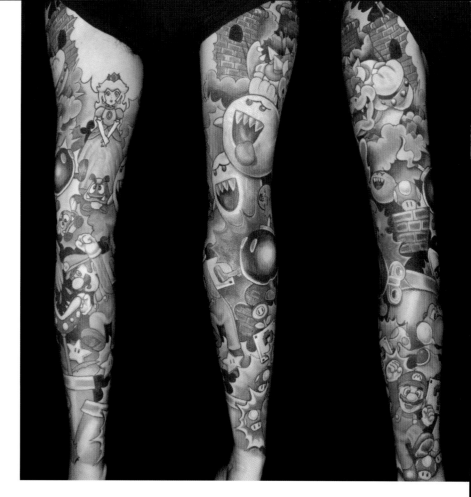

FACING PAGE:
All images: clean lines, a carefully controlled palette and graphic representations are the hallmark of French artist Noon of Boucherie Traditionnelle, France.

THIS PAGE:
RIGHT
Tattoos inspired by a nostalgia for 1980s graphics, by Arran Burton of Cosmic Tattoo, Colchester, UK.

BELOW
Recently revived for a new generation, Super Mario still occupies a special place in the hearts of those who played the game in its 1980s heyday. Tattoo by Tommi of No Regrets, Cheltenham, UK.

BELOW RIGHT
Looney Tunes fandom is evident in this colourful, humorous sleeve by Marcus of All Style Tattoo, Berlin, Germany.

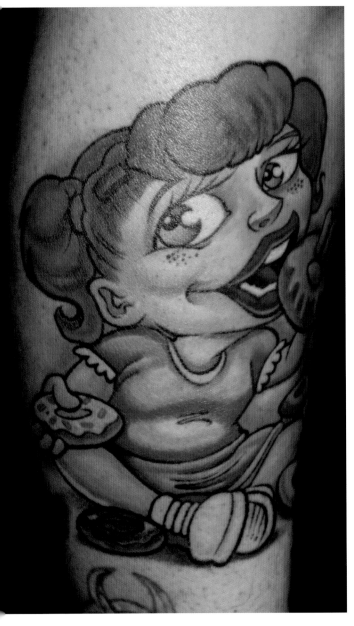

TOP LEFT
Cartoon girl eating doughnuts by Tony Ciavarro of Stinky Monkey, Kingston, Massachusetts, USA.

TOP RIGHT
Candy-coloured startled owl tattoo by Jessi Manchester of All Style Tattoo, Berlin, Germany.

BELOW LEFT
My Little Pony chest piece by Christina of Mystery Touch, Gleisdorf, Austria.

BELOW RIGHT
Some of us never grow out of childhood toys! My Little Pony reaches kitsch icon status in this tattoo by Doc Fell of Mike's Tattoos, Carlisle, UK.

ABOVE
A big-eyed rubber duck bath plug by Alex of Sandor Haraszti, Hungary.

ABOVE RIGHT
Screaming snowman tattoo by Bez of Triplesix Studios, Sunderland, UK.

BOTTOM LEFT
From modelling clay to cartoon and then tattoo art! Wallace and Gromit tattoo by Katy of Liquorice Tattoo, Kirriesmuir, Scotland, UK.

FAR RIGHT
A tribute to mama's home-cooked doughnuts, or something more saucy? You decide! Tattoo by Fabio Moro of Moro Tattoo, Genoa, Italy.

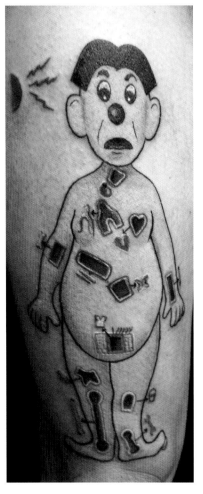

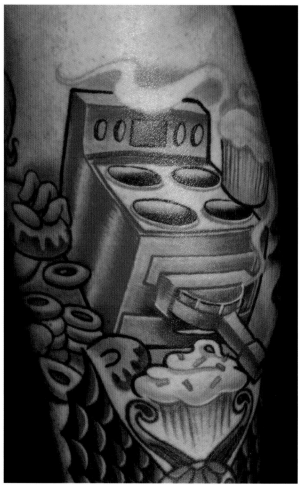

FACING PAGE:
TOP
Judging by his body art, this chef takes his job very seriously! Tattoo by Leah Moule of Spear Studio, Birmingham, UK.

BOTTOM LEFT
Manufactured since 1965, the battery-operated hospital game Operation now has cult status. Tattoo by Fabio Moro of Moro Tattoo, Genoa, Italy.

CENTRE
The Swedish chef from the Muppets, by Enrico of Spunk Tattoo, Italy.

BOTTOM RIGHT
Baking cupcakes tattoo by Tony Ciavarro of Stinky Monkey, Kingston, Massachusetts, USA.

THIS PAGE:
TOP LEFT
A rag doll chef-DJ mixes with a kitchen glove. Childish crayon techniques are blended with simple graphics. Tattoo by Moro, Moro Tattoo, Genoa, Italy.

TOP RIGHT
Charcoal sketch tattoo by Nico of Steel Workshop, Fribourg, Switzerland.

BOTTOM LEFT
A fun tattoo that can be viewed both ways up, by Kris Domanowski of Plus 48, Edinburgh, UK.

BOTTOM RIGHT
Like an old photo, but with a weird twist. Tattoo by Mark of Global Tattoo, Wirral, UK.

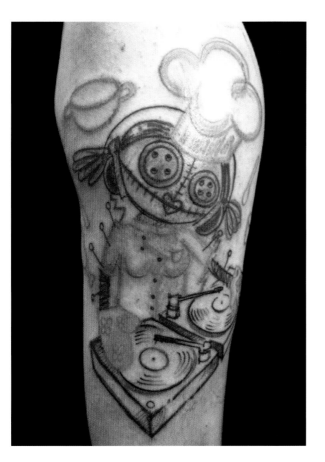

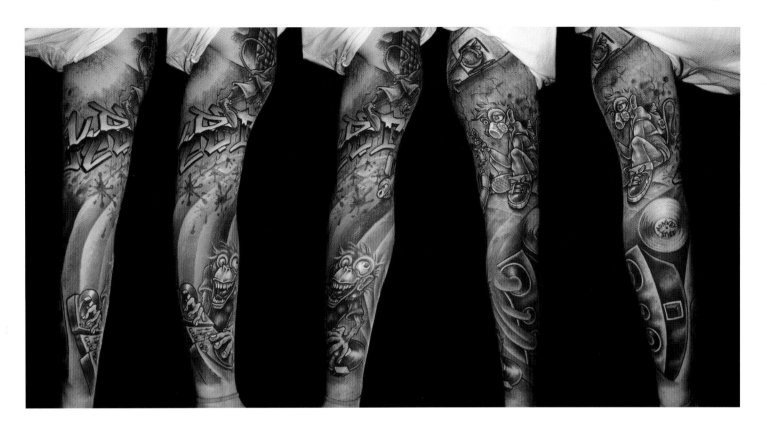

FACING PAGE:

TOP LEFT
An imaginative robotic vision by Kris Domanowski of Plus 48, Edinburgh, UK.

TOP RIGHT
A psychedelic snail with building plans! Humorous tattoo by Anabi of Anabi Tattoo, Szczecin, Poland.

BOTTOM LEFT
A skewed and imaginatively simple tattoo on a London theme by Noon of Boucherie Traditionnelle, France.

BOTTOM RIGHT
Adapted from an original painting by pop-surrealist artist Mark Ryden, this tattoo is by Mirek Vel Stotker of Stotker Tattoo, London.

THIS PAGE:

TOP
A phantasmagoric homage to DJ and graffiti culture by Krzysztof Domanowski of Plus 48, Edinburgh, UK.

ABOVE
Gorgeous colours in this image of a nurse fawn coming to the aid of woodland friends. Tattoo by Miss Nico of All Style Tattoo, Berlin, Germany.

LEFT
You can't fight your natural instincts! Cartoon styling and colour add humour to this St Bernard's failed rescue mission. Tattoo by Alessandro of Los Tres Ases, Cerdanyola del Vallés, Spain.

THIS PAGE:
ABOVE
Strong contour lines and colours in this humorous retelling of the Aladdin story, by Daveee of Kult Tattoo, Krakow, Poland.

BOTTOM
Family Guy character Peter Griffin with his indefatigable nemesis. Tattoo by Carlos Rojas of Black Inker Collective, Esperia, California, USA.

FACING PAGE:
TOP LEFT
A spiky character inspired by graffiti art by Mark Bailey of Golden Dragon, Chester, UK.

RIGHT
A tortured clown in the spotlight. Tattoo by Irene Thill of One More Tattoo, Luxembourg.

BOTTOM LEFT
A Joker image inspired by Jack Nicholson's interpretation of the role. Tattoo by Josu Franzh of Original Tattoo, Barcelona, Spain.

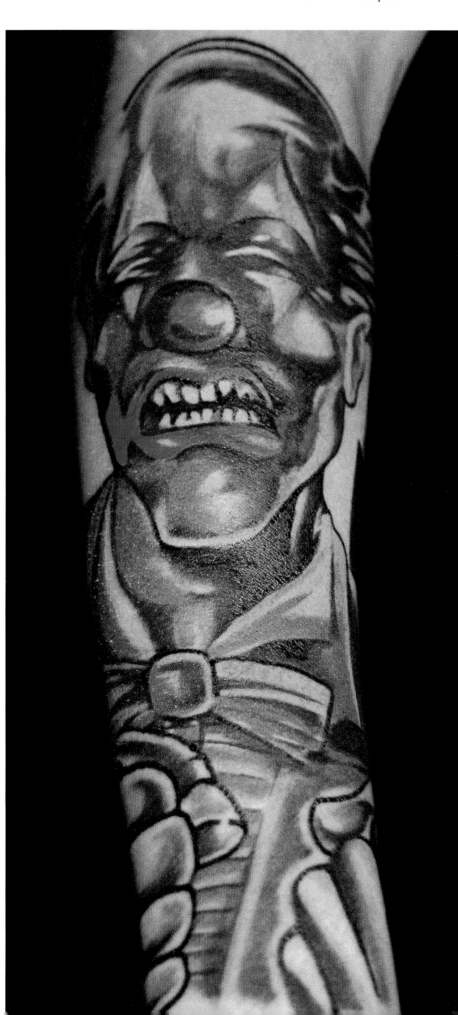

SYMBOLISM

Having a tattoo is a strong personal statement, so it is not surprising that some of the most popular tattoo subjects are symbols with potent meanings. The choice is seemingly limitless, from pantheistic sun, star and zodiac designs to Celtic, Maori, Haida and Kanji motifs. Symbols suggest different things to different people and their meanings may alter over time. The more abstract the tattoo, the easier it is for people to ascribe their own interpretation to the image.

People get a tattoo for a range of reasons: to mark a particular time in their lives, to remember someone, to ward off bad luck, to make a political or religious statement, to celebrate and embrace ancient symbols of power, survival and rebirth or to create new ones. Symbols that are loaded with significance for one person may be completely meaningless to another individual.

Tattoos have been imbued with deep meaning ever since people first started putting ink on their skin. In certain societies, tattoos are not just decorative, but carry great social significance. In the Maori culture, for example, tattoos indicate the wearer's standing in the community, as well as their status and courage. Outside such communities, tattoos are widely used to denote affiliation to a specific group, or as a public declaration of a commitment or an achievement.

FACING PAGE: A stunning back piece inspired by Egyptian iconography, by Florence Amblard, Galérie d'Art, Paris, France.

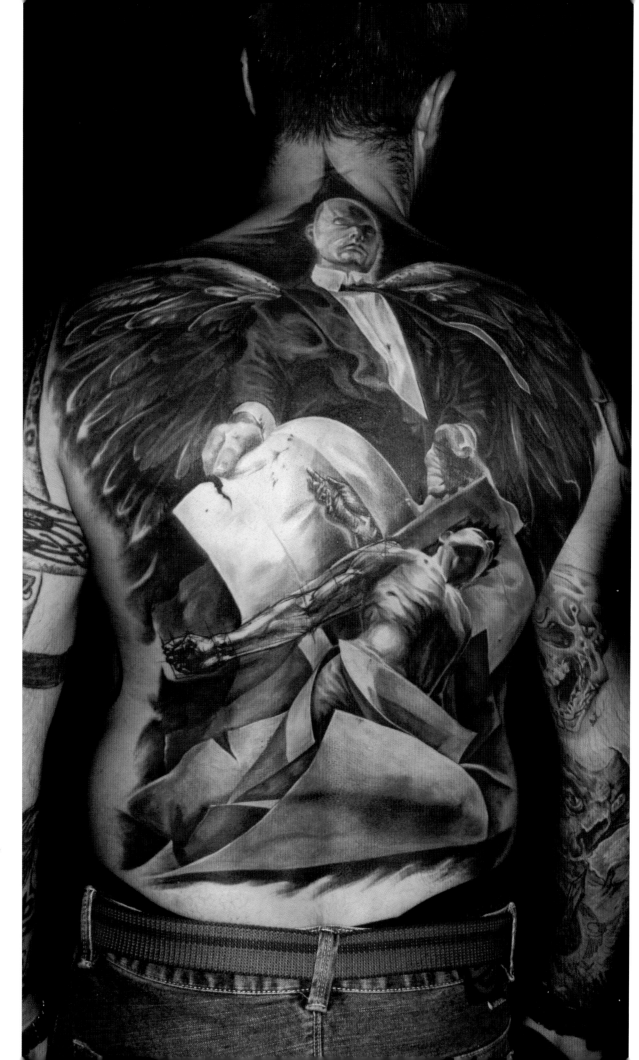

FACING PAGE:

TOP LEFT
The Statue of Liberty with an image of Marilyn Monroe brandishing a machine gun superimposed. Tattoo by José Antonio Bandera of Soul Hunter.

TOP RIGHT
Timid manga child by Derek Young of Yankee Tattoos, Dundee, UK.

BOTTOM LEFT
A surreal back piece inspired by artist Salvador Dali. Tattoo by Andy Bowler of Monki Do, Belper, UK.

BOTTOM RIGHT
An apocalyptic war scene in subtly nuanced black and grey by Dan Banas of Bananas Tattoo, Formby, UK.

THIS PAGE:
A reinterpretation of the Faustian pact by Bartosz of Caffeine Tattoo, Warsaw, Poland.

FACING PAGE:
An urban angel image, beautifully inked by Miss Nico of All Style Tattoo, Berlin, Germany.

THIS PAGE:
TOP LEFT
The gold and precious stones of Tutankhamun's burial mask are expertly rendered by Anabi of Anabi Tattoo, Szczecin, Poland.

TOP RIGHT
This bas-relief piece is influenced by Ancient Egyptian symbolism. Tattoo by Robert Kornajzel of One More Tattoo, Luxembourg.

BOTTOM LEFT
The owl symbolizes wisdom and protection and in certain cultures also represents the occult. This owl carries a heart. Tattoo by Sam Ricketts of Jayne Doe, Hornchurch, Essex, UK.

BOTTOM RIGHT
A black-and-grey phoenix, symbol of rebirth and regeneration by JPeine Tattoo, Madrid, Spain.

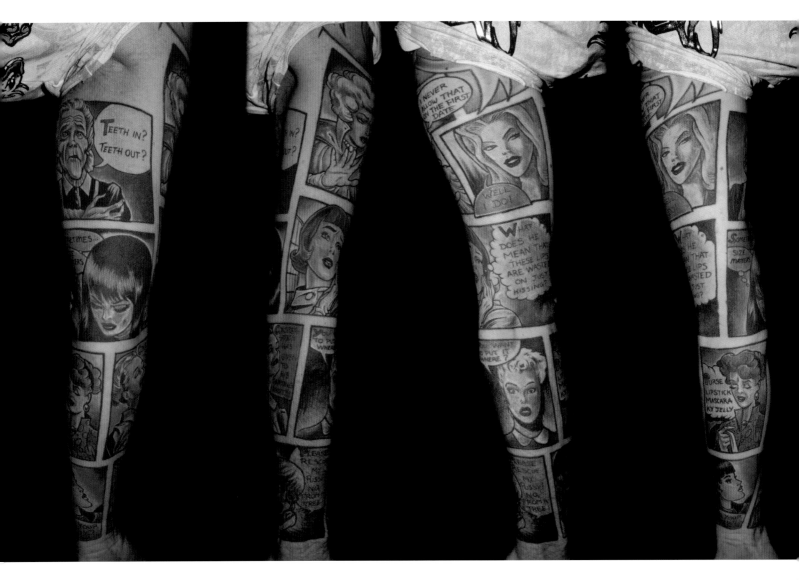

FACING PAGE:
TOP
A comic strip about dating. Tattoo by Woody of Woody's Tattoo Studio, High Wycombe, UK.

BOTTOM
A Roy Lichtenstein-inspired comic strip. Tattoo by Sonya of Reds Tattoo Parlour, Essex, UK.

THIS PAGE:
TOP
Tattoo based on a storyboard for a cowboy movie, by Jessi Manchester of All Style Tattoo, Berlin, Germany.

BOTTOM
A comic strip in black and grey, eye-catching and starkly lit. Tattoo by Chris Hatton of Physical Graffiti, Cardiff, UK.

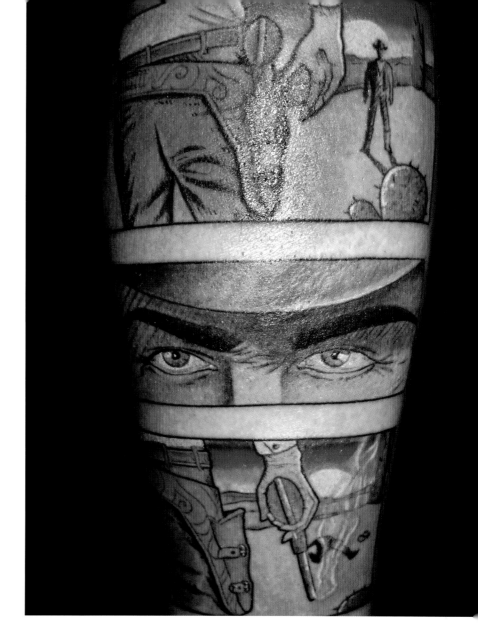

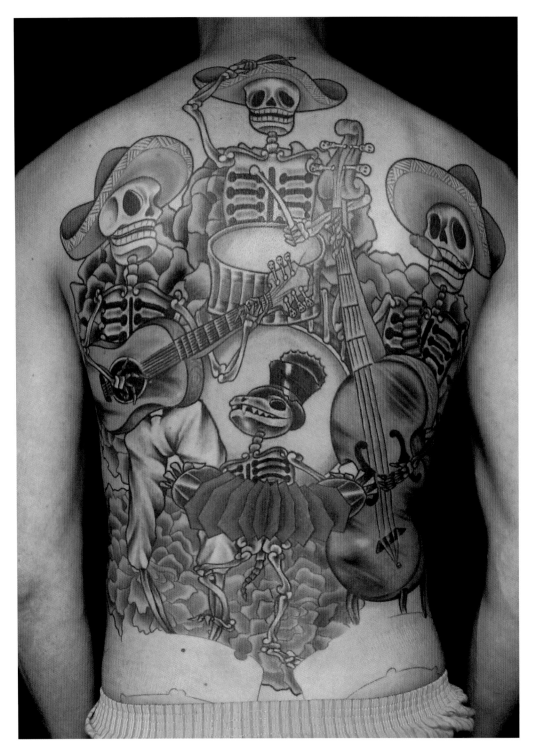

THIS PAGE:
ABOVE
Mexican Day of the Dead treatment of a mariachi band. Tattoo by Jan of Für Immer, Berlin, Germany.

TOP RIGHT
A macabre interpretation of the traditional matryoshka doll by Adam Nelson, Nelson Ink Tattoo Harrogate, UK.

BOTTOM RIGHT
Cunning, fast and savage – a wolf in disguise carries a skull in its mouth. Tattoo by Hik of Exotic Tattoo, Murcia, Spain.

FACING PAGE:
An imposing back piece packed with symbols commenting on American culture, power and politics. Tattoo by Fernando of Forever Tattoo, Puerto Sagunto, Valencia, Spain.

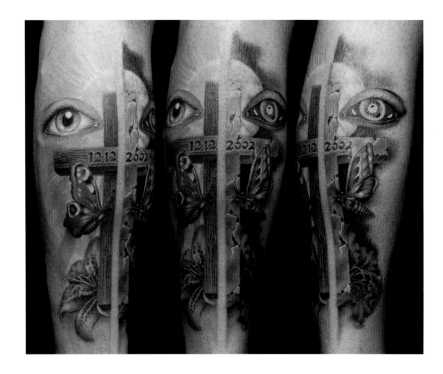

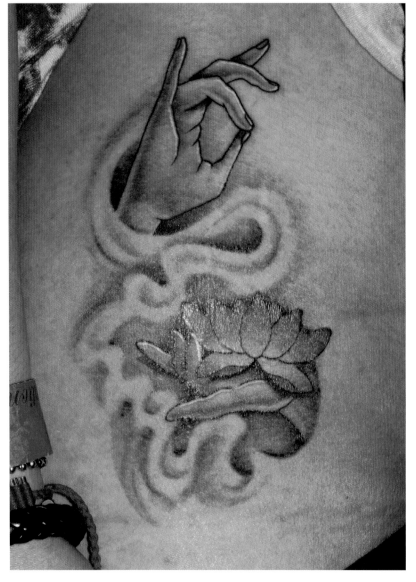

TOP LEFT
A memorial tattoo by Miss Nico of All Style Tattoo, Berlin, Germany.

ABOVE
Obsolete gaming consoles and pixellated games heroes signify nostalgia for lost youth. Tattoo by Mark Gibson of Monki Do, Belper, UK.

LEFT
A delicate tattoo of a pair of hands. The lotus flower is a potent symbol in Buddhist, Hindu and Ancient Egyptian cultures. Tattoo by Leigh Oldcorn of Cosmic Tattoo, Colchester, UK.

FACING PAGE:
This striking image of the Virgin Mary and the infant Jesus has bold colours and makes good use of the human canvas. Tattoo by George Mavridis of Tattooligans, Thessaloniki, Greece.

FACING PAGE:
FAR LEFT
An anthropomorphized cat with symbols galore! Tattoo by Inma, London and Brighton, UK.

TOP RIGHT
A brightly coloured yet sinister jester's mask by Hayley Hayes of Self Preservation Custom Tattoo Studio, Amersham, UK.

CENTRE RIGHT
A smiling sliver of moon, graffiti-style by Robin of Planet Tattoo, Czech Republic.

BOTTOM RIGHT
Halloween motifs by Gray Silva of Rampant Ink, Nottingham, UK.

THIS PAGE:
TOP
The businessman and the rain cloud image symbolize a desire to break free from the monotony of working life. Tattoo by Fabio Moro of Moro Tattoo, Genoa, Italy.

ABOVE
Surreal, fun and highly individual artwork and tattoo by Noon of Boucherie Traditionnelle, France.

RIGHT
An imaginative, stylized tattoo with precise geometric patterns, by Noon of Boucherie Traditionnelle, France.

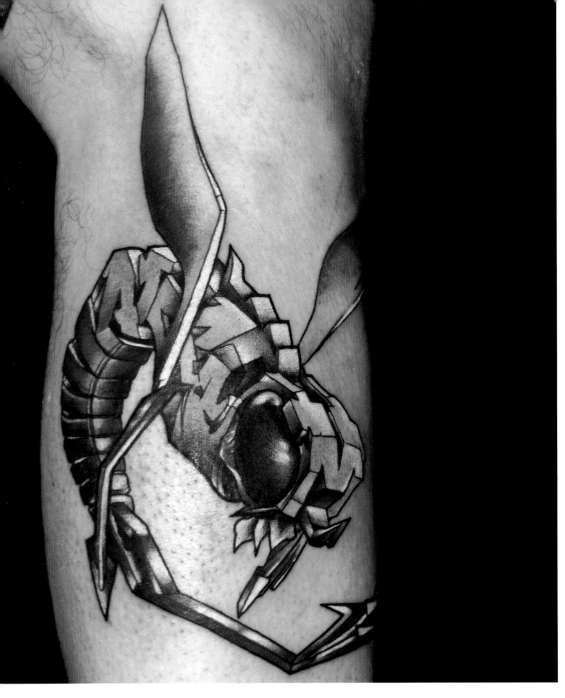

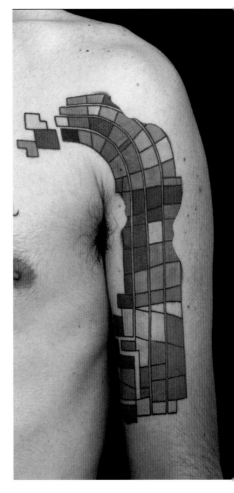

TOP LEFT
A robotic wasp with a threatening sting.
Tattoo by Andy Bowler of Monki Do,
Belper, UK.

ABOVE
Fragmented mosaic tattoo by Avishai Tene
of Ink Junkies, Luxembourg.

LEFT
A universal messbrille, an optometrist's
tool rendered with precise tattooing
by Yliana Paolini of One More Tattoo,
Luxembourg.

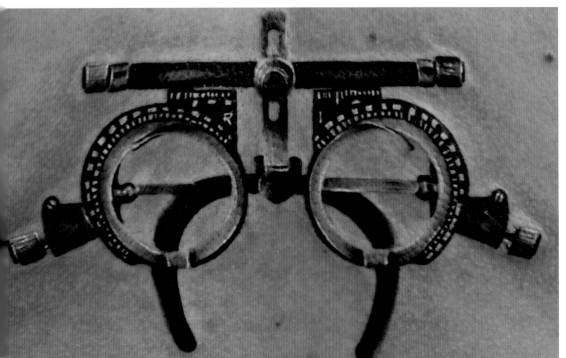

ABOVE
A Cubist rendering of labourers at an ironworks. Tattoo by Bugs of Los Angeles, California, USA.

RIGHT
A zombie representation of Hello Kitty by Anabi of Anabi Tattoo, Szczecin, Poland.

FAR RIGHT
Origami instructions and final results. Tattoo by Jessi Manchester of All Style Tattoo, Berlin, Germany.

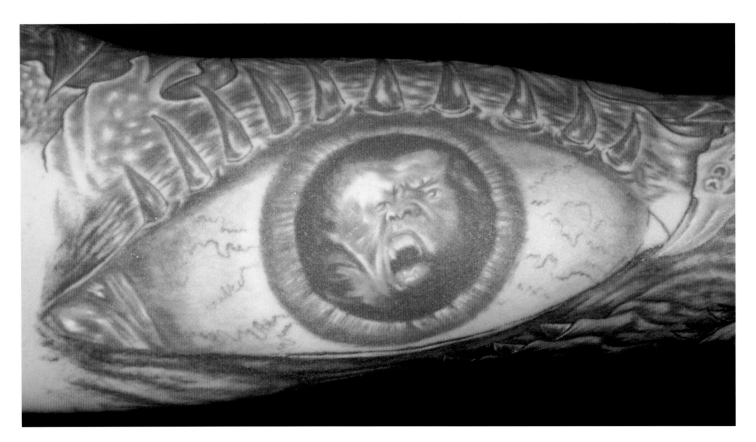

THIS PAGE:
ABOVE
Primate scream: an ape seen through a human eye in extreme close up. Tattoo by Benjamin of Tom's Tattoo World, Graz, Austria.

FAR LEFT
Native American chief tattoo by Robert Kornajzel of One More Tattoo, Luxembourg.

LEFT
In memoriam tattoo by Jez Bradley.

FACING PAGE:
Green mice and alien imaginings by one of Poland's top artists, Tofi of Inkognito, Rybnik.

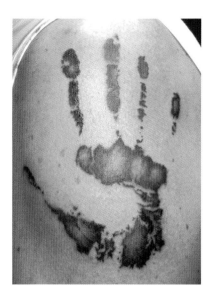

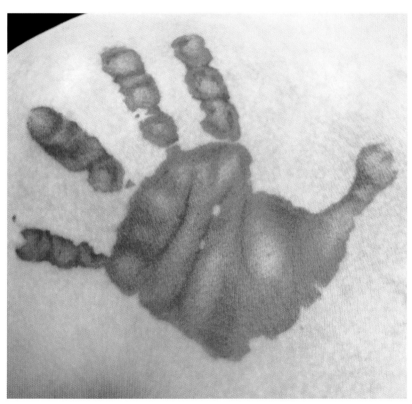

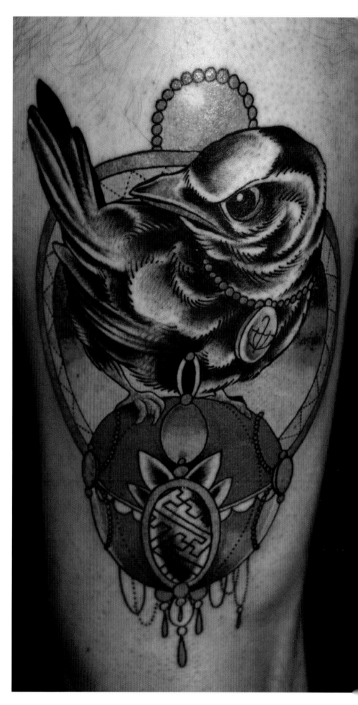

FACING PAGE:
TOP
An imposing crowned owl symbol by Nervio, Roses and Panthers, Mexico.

BOTTOM
Traditional tattoo icons including roses, skulls, anchors and gemstones work well together in this large piece that still manages to leave a lot of skin bare. Tattoo by Emily Hansen of World of Tattoos, Ruislip Manor, UK.

THIS PAGE:
TOP AND BOTTOM LEFT
Hand-print tattoos by Tanya Buxton of Monki Do, Belper, UK.

TOP CENTRE
Sands of time tattoo by Jim Minor of Analogue Tattoos, California, USA.

ABOVE
Bejewelled bird by Stu Pagdin, Whitstable, Kent, UK.

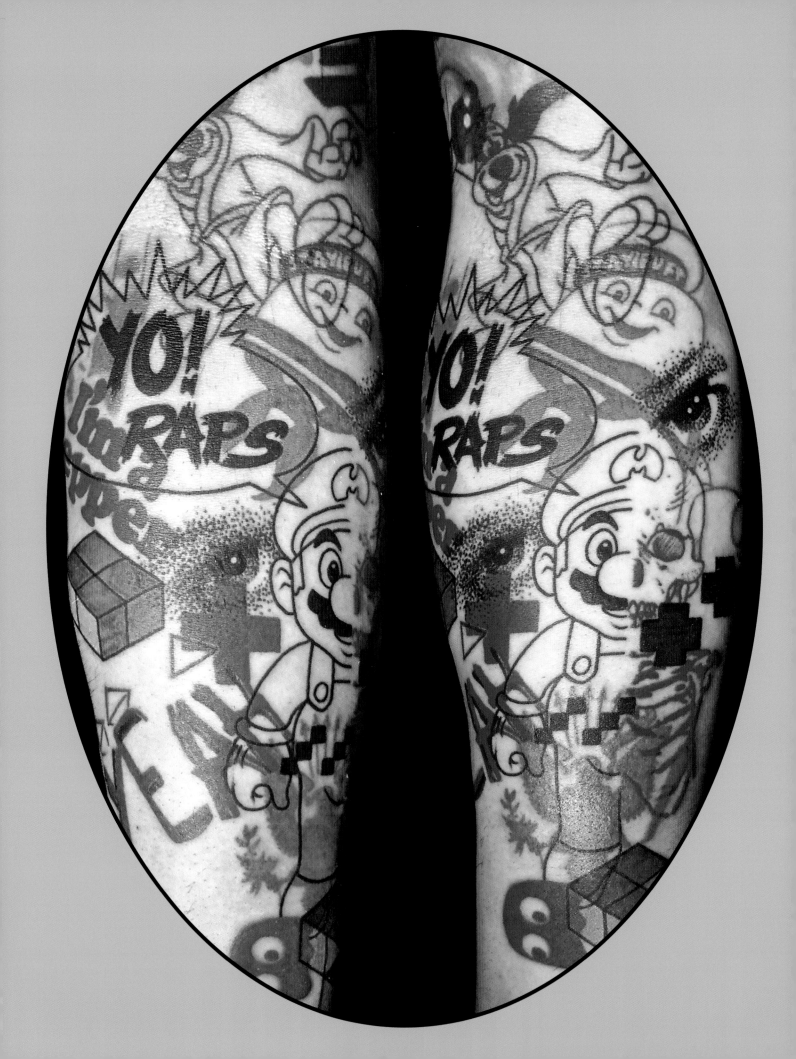

FUSION

There is a new generation of tattoo artists who have honed their skills not by the art school route or via traditional apprenticeships but through other visual disciplines such as graphic design, sculpture, illustration, graffiti art and photography. These artists bring a fresh, often unorthodox approach to the practice of tattooing, opening up new possibilities for the medium.

Some of the most inventive tattoo artwork I have seen is by artists such as Volko and Simone from Buena Vista Tattoo Club, or Jef Palumbo from Boucherie Moderne, practitioners who have developed their skills while working for corporate clients in other media. These artists combine different techniques to achieve their distinctive custom-made tattoos. Using lines, blocks of colour, paint strokes, worn lettering, assorted typefaces, photographic, photocopying and sketching styles, they layer various effects to produce tattoos that are resolutely modern in feel.

These artists have pushed the boundaries and changed the perception of what a tattoo should look like. But not all the images in this chapter rely on graphic solutions. Fusion means mixing different styles, and there are examples here of tattoos where modern and traditional ideas are merged to create something entirely fresh and new.

FACING PAGE: A wonderful example of mixed visual media tattooed onto skin as if in layers. Tattoo by Jef Palumbo of Boucherie Moderne, Brussels, Belgium.

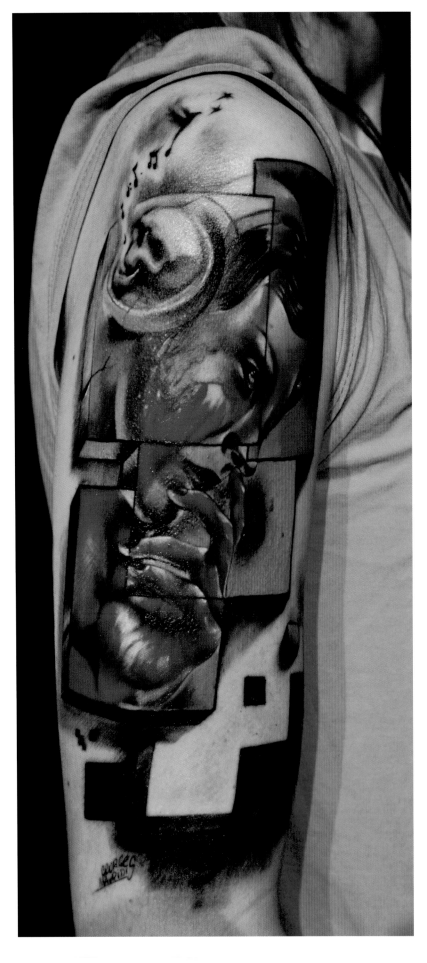

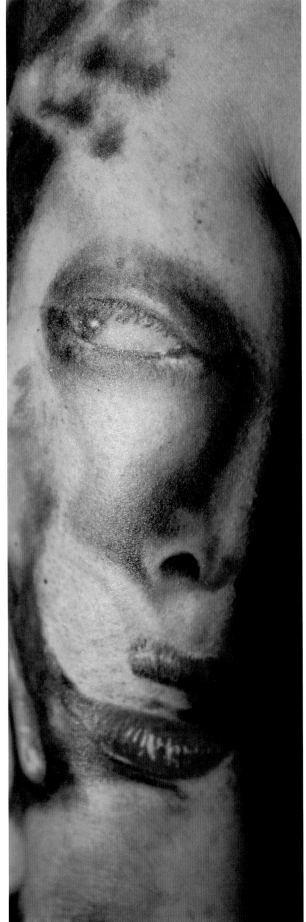

FACING PAGE:
FAR LEFT
A deconstructed, multi-layered portrait by George Mavridis of Tattooligans, Thessaloniki, Greece.

LEFT
A detailed photo-realistic close-up with smoke. Tattoo by Thanassis of Erevos Creations, Greece.

THIS PAGE:
This striking tattoo follows photographic convention by depicting part of the image out of focus. Increasingly, shallow depth of field is being used by artists of photo-realistic tattoos. Tattoo by Thanassis of Erevos Creations, Greece.

FACING PAGE:
TOP
A large tribal motif reveals a photo-realistic wolf portrait. Tattoo by Robert Kornajzel of One More Tattoo, Luxembourg.

BOTTOM
An apocalyptic vision: splashes of red paint give this black and grey tattoo plenty of movement. Tattoo by Miss Nico of All Style Tattoo, Berlin, Germany.

THIS PAGE:
A traditional geisha scene with a difference: the wearer's skin appears to have been slashed to reveal the muscles beneath. Tattoo by Miss Nico of All Style Tattoo, Berlin, Germany.

THIS PAGE:
A skull made up of tropical motifs such as palm trees, exotic flowers, boats and ocean scenes. Tattoo by Andy Engel of Andy's Tattoo, Kitzingen, Germany.

FACING PAGE:
LEFT
A mixture of graphics, photo-realism and abstract art. Tattoo by Miss Nico of All Style Tattoo, Berlin, Germany.

RIGHT
A complex tattoo made up of graphic elements, using only black and red ink. Tattoo by Jef Palumbo of Boucherie Moderne, Brussels, Belgium.

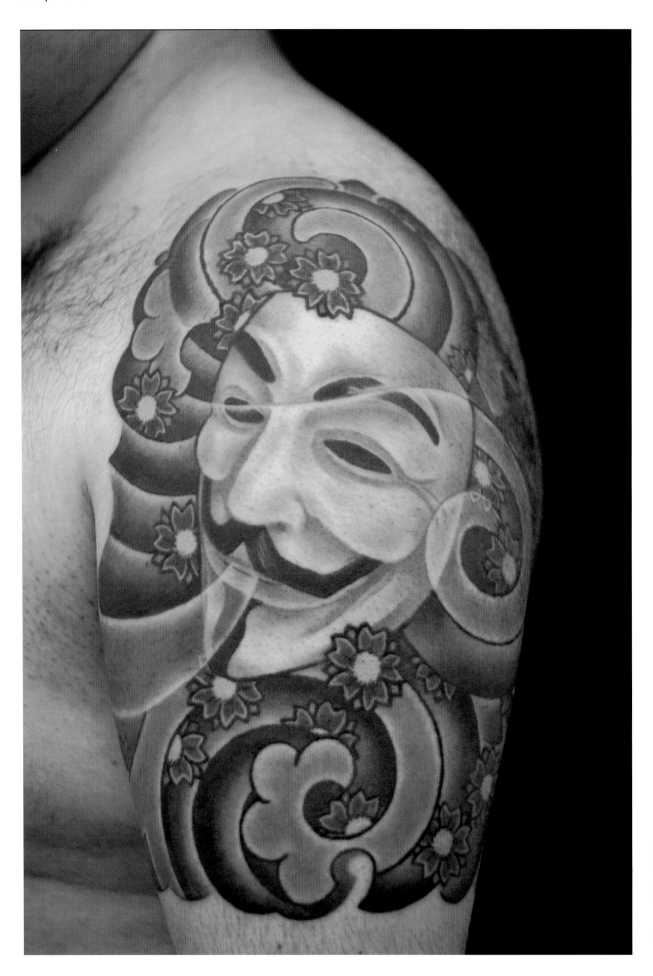

LEFT
Oriental motifs frame this version of the well-known 'V for Vendetta' mask. Tattoo by Avishai Tene of Ink Junkies, Luxembourg.

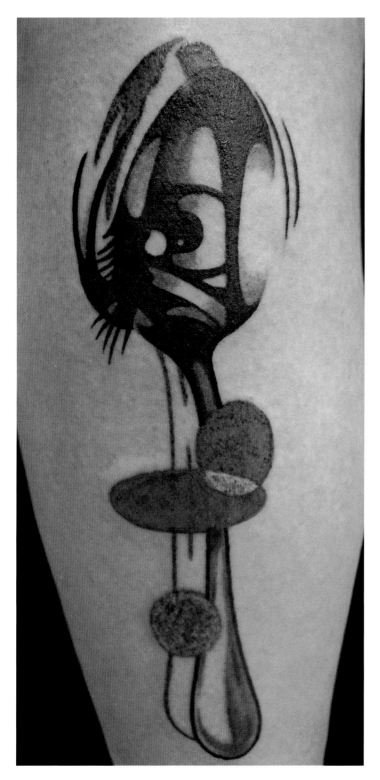
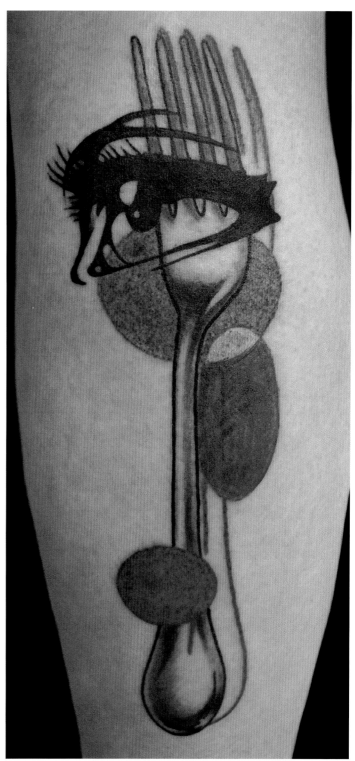

ABOVE
Cutlery symbols
get the pop art
treatment. Tattoos
by Jef Palumbo
of Boucherie
Moderne,
Brussels, Belgium.

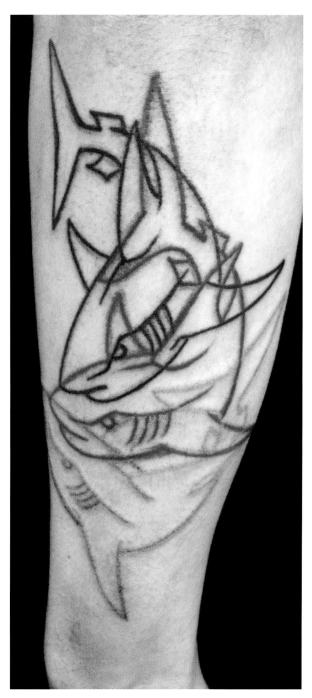

FACING PAGE:
A large black-and-white tattoo reminiscent of street artist JR's work, this image disintegrates into round pixels. Tattoo by Jessi Manchester of All Style Tattoo, Berlin, Germany.

THIS PAGE:
LEFT
A flowery, almost romantic representation of a woman's face with pixels and smears of black ink. Tattoo by Jef of Boucherie Moderne, Brussels, Belgium.

RIGHT
The outline of a shark superimposed in different positions and colours has an almost 3D effect. Tattoo by Fabio Moro of Moro Tattoo, Genoa, Italy.

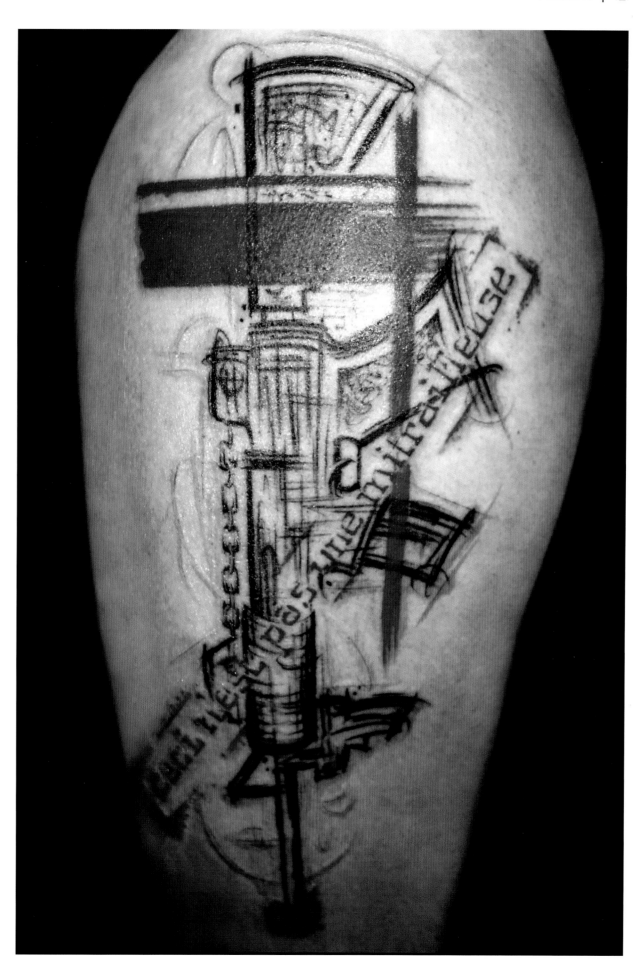

FACING PAGE:
A mixture of tribal patterns and stylized red flames distinguishes this crossover piece. Tattoo by Jan of Für Immer, Berlin, Germany.

THIS PAGE:
A submachine gun with 'typed' lettering and bold lines gives this artwork a sketch-like feel. Tattoo by Jessi Manchester of All Style Tattoo, Berlin, Germany.

CREDITS

Thanks to:

Anabi, Andy Engel, Araceli Old Skull 4ever, Avishai Tene,

Andy Bowler, Boff Konkerz, Fabio Moro, Florence Amblard, Für Immer,

Jef Palumbo, Jo Harrison, Leo, Liorcifer, Magda Zon, Marion Thill,

Miss Nico, Nicola Bevan, Noon, Sakrosankt, Tessa Rose, Tracy D

PICTURE ACKNOWLEDGEMENTS

Half title page: tattoo by Jan of Für Immer

Facing title page: tattoo by Andy Engel of Andy's Tattoo

Title page: tattoo by Leo of Naked Trust

Imprint page: tattoo by Jessi of All Style Tattoo, Berlin, Germany

This page, right: tattoo by Mark Gibson of Monki Do

Links:

All Style Tattoo · · · · · · · · · · · · · · · · · · · http://www.allstyle-tattoo.de/

Anabi Tattoo · http://www.anabi-tattoo.com/

Andy Engel, Andy's Tattoo · · · · · · · · · · http://www.andys-tattoo.com/en/

Avishai Tene, Ink Junkies · · · · · · · · · · · http://www.inkjunkies.com/

Boff Konkerz, Roadmaps for the Soul · · · http://www.roadmapsforthesoul.com/about-boff-konkerz/

Cosmic Tattoo · · · · · · · · · · · · · · · · · · · http://www.cosmictattoo.com/

Cult Classic Tattoo · · · · · · · · · · · · · · · · http://www.cultclassictattoo.co.uk/

Florence Amblard, Galerie d'Art · · · · · · · http://www.tatouage-art-paris.fr/

Für Immer · http://www.fuerimmertattoo.de/

George Mavridis, Tattooligans · · · · · · · · http://www.tattooligans.com/studio/

Jef, Boucherie Moderne · · · · · · · · · · · · http://www.boucheriemoderne.be/

Jo Harrison, Modern Body Art · · · · · · · · http://modernbodyart.co.uk/

Leo, Naked Trust · · · · · · · · · · · · · · · · · http://www.nakedtrust.com/

Liorcifer, Tribulation Tattoo · · · · · · · · · http://www.tribulationtattoo.com/Home.aspx

Monki Do · http://www.monkido.net/

Moro Tattoo · http://www.morotattoo.com/

Noon, Boucherie Traditionnelle · · · · · · · http://boucherie-traditionnelle.com/

One More Tattoo · · · · · · · · · · · · · · · · · http://www.tattoo.lu/

Sakrosankt · http://www.sakrosankt.com/

13 Diamonds · http://www.13diamonds.com/

V Tattoo · http://www.vtattoo.es/